P8 - BZC - 187

BEFORE & AFTER
SOCRATES

BEFORE AND AFTER SOCRATES

BY

FRANCIS MACDONALD
CORNFORD

CAMBRIDGE
AT THE UNIVERSITY PRESS

PUBLISHED BY
THE SYNDICS OF THE CAMBRIDGE UNIVERSITY PRESS

Bentley House, 200 Euston Road, London. N.W. 1
American Branch: 32 East 57th Street, New York 22, N.Y.

First edition	1932
Reprinted	1950
Reprinted (twice)	1960
Reprinted (twice)	1962
	1964
	1965
	1966
	1968
	1972
	1974

———

PRINTED IN THE U.S.A.

IN MEMORY OF
GOLDSWORTHY LOWES DICKINSON

CONTENTS

PREFACE

A student in any branch of knowledge who is invited to set before a popular audience, within the space of four hours, the gist and upshot of his studies,[1] may do well to submit himself to the discipline implied. He knows that the expert will frown upon some of his statements as questionable in content and dogmatic in tone, and will mark the omission of many things for which no room could be found. But it will do him good to sit back in his chair and look for the main outline, so often obscured by detail. It seemed clear that Socrates must be taken as the central figure in the period allotted to me, and that my business was to convey the significance of his conversion of philosophy from the study of Nature to the study of human life. I have tried, accordingly, so to describe the early Ionian science as to show why it failed to satisfy Socrates,

[1] The four lectures contained in this book were delivered as part of a course on Greek Philosophy at the Summer Meeting arranged by the Board of Extra-Mural Studies at Cambridge in August, 1932. The subject chosen for the Meeting was The Contribution of Ancient Greece to Modern Life.

and I have treated the systems of Plato and Aristotle as attempts to carry into the interpretation of the world the consequences of Socrates' discovery. I have gained a fuller understanding of that discovery from M. Henri Bergson's book, *Les deux sources de la morale et de la religion*, which came into my hands when I was meditating these lectures.

Just before delivering the last of the series I heard of the death of Goldsworthy Lowes Dickinson, the wise and gentle humanist who had been well chosen to inaugurate our study of the contribution of Greece to modern life. No English scholar has better shown, by what he was even more than by what he wrote, how, in a world that sometimes seems to have forgotten more than it has learnt since Athens fell, the spirit of Socrates can live again.

F.M.C.

August, 1932

Chapter I

IONIAN SCIENCE BEFORE SOCRATES

In this course of lectures it falls to me to speak of the whole creative period of Greek philosophy—of the Ionian science of Nature before Socrates, of Socrates himself, and of his chief followers, Plato and his pupil Aristotle. I cannot attempt even a bare outline of the history of thought in a period covering nearly three centuries, the sixth, fifth, and fourth, before our era. I shall only try to explain why the life and work of Socrates stand out as marking the central crisis or turning-point in that history. We speak of the pre-Socratics, then of Socrates, and finally of the Socratic philosophy elaborated by Plato and Aristotle. Why should the name of Socrates be used to describe the philosophy that came before him as well as the philosophy that came after?

Plato in one of his dialogues has made Socrates himself describe the revolution of thought he effected—how he turned philosophy from the study of external Nature to the study of man and of the purposes of human action in society. In the *Phaedo*, the conversation between Socrates and his friends on the day of his death reaches the question whether the soul is a thing of the sort that can begin and cease to exist. This question calls for a review of the explanations that had been given of the becoming and perishing of transitory things. Let me recall the substance of that famous passage.

Socrates begins by saying that in his youth he had been eager to learn how philosophers had accounted for the origin of the world and of living creatures. He soon gave up this science of Nature, because he could not be satisfied with the sort of explanations or reasons offered. Some, for instance, had found the origin of life in a process of fermentation set up by the action of heat and cold. Socrates felt that such explanations left him none the wiser, and he concluded that he had no natural talent for inquiries of this sort.

We can infer from the sequel why he was dissatisfied. In this earlier science a physical event was supposed to be 'explained' when it was (so to say) taken to pieces and described in terms of other physical events preceding or composing it. Such an explanation offers a more detailed picture of *how* the event came about; it does not, Socrates thought, tell us *why* it came about. The kind of reason Socrates wanted was the reason why.

Socrates then heard someone reading aloud a book by Anaxagoras, the philosophic friend of

Pericles, which said that the world had been ordered by an Intelligence. This raised his hopes to a high pitch. An Intelligence ordering all things will surely, he thought, dispose them 'for the best'. He expected to find that Anaxagoras would explain the world order as a work of design, not a result of blind mechanical necessity. The reason of that order would then be found, not in some previous state of things from which it had emerged, but in some end or purpose that it could be shown to serve. Reasons of that sort seemed to Socrates intelligible and satisfying. Why was he at that moment sitting in prison awaiting death? Not because the muscles in his body had contracted in a certain way to carry him there and place him in a sitting posture; but because his mind had thought it better to abide the sentence of the Athenian court. On reading Anaxagoras, however, Socrates found that the action of this Intelligence was limited to starting motion in space; and for the rest Anaxagoras fell back on mechanical causes of the usual type. In this system the world, after all, was not designed for any good purpose. Socrates himself could not do what Anaxagoras had left undone. He gave up all hope of an intelligible system of Nature, and turned away from the study of external things.

Accordingly, we find the Socrates depicted by Plato and Xenophon conversing, not about Nature, but about human life in society, the meaning of right and wrong, the ends for which we ought to live.

Plato has here described something of far deeper significance than a critical moment in the biography of Socrates. It was not only the man Socrates, but philosophy itself that turned, in his person, from the outer to the inner world. Up to that moment, the eyes of philosophy had been turned outwards to seek a reasonable explanation of the shifting spectacle of surrounding Nature. Now their vision is directed to another field— the order and purposes of human life—and, at the centre of that field, to the nature of the individual soul. Pre-Socratic philosophy begins (as I shall try to show) with the discovery of Nature; Socratic philosophy begins with the discovery of man's soul.

The life of Socrates found its appropriate motto in the Delphic inscription, 'Know thyself'. Why was it that, just at that time and place, man discovered in himself a problem of more pressing importance than the understanding of external Nature? We might have expected that philosophy should begin at home, with the understanding that man's own soul and the meaning of his own life are more to him than the natural history of lifeless things. Why did man study Nature first, and forget the need to know himself till Socrates proclaimed that need as his chief concern? To find an answer to that question, we must now consider the early Ionian science of Nature, its character, and how it arose.

This science is called 'Ionian' because it was begun by Thales and his successors at Miletus, one of the Ionian colonies on the coast of Asia Minor. Thales lived at the beginning of the sixth century. The development of Ionian science culminated two centuries later in the Atomism of Democritus, a contemporary of Socrates and Plato.

All the histories of Greek philosophy, from Aristotle's time to this day, begin with Thales of Miletus. It is generally agreed that with him something new, that we call Western science, appeared in the world—science as commonly defined: the pursuit of knowledge for its own sake, not for any practical use it can be made to serve. Thales, travelling in the East, found that the Egyptians possessed some rough rules of land measurement. Every year the inundation of the Nile obliterated the landmarks, and the peasants' fields had to be marked out afresh. The Egyptians had a method of calculating rectangular areas, and so solved their practical problem. The inquisitive Greek was not interested in marking out fields. He saw that the method could be detached from that particular purpose and generalised into a method of calculating areas of any shape. So the rules of land measurement were converted into the science of geometry. The problem—something to be done—gave place to the theorem—something to be contemplated. Reason found a fresh delight in knowing that the angles at the base of an isosceles triangle are always equal, and why they must be equal. The land surveyor still makes use of this truth in constructing maps; the philosopher is content to enjoy it because it is true.

In the same way the Greeks turned the art of astrology into the science of astronomy. For many centuries the Babylonian priests had recorded the movements of the planets, in order to predict human events, which the stars were believed to govern. The Greeks borrowed the results of observation, and Thales predicted an eclipse which occurred in Asia Minor in 585 B.C. But they ignored the whole fabric of astrological superstition which had hitherto provided the practical motive for observing the heavens. There is hardly a trace of astrology in Greek thought before the fusion of East and West following the conquests of Alexander.

The rise of science, then, meant that the intelligence became disinterested and now felt free to voyage on seas of thought strange to minds bent on immediate problems of action. Reason sought and found truth that was universal, but might, or might not, be useful for the exigencies of life. Looking back across some 2500 years, we see the cosmogonies of the Milesian School as the dawn or infancy of science. Here the histories of philosophy start, after a few remarks on the earlier age of mythology and superstition. But, for our purpose of appreciating the Socratic revolution of thought, it will be useful to look at this starting-point of philosophy from the other side—the farther side. If we could survey the whole development of mankind, these last twenty-five centuries of science from Thales to our own day would appear in a very different proportion and perspective. We should then see philosophy as the latest of man's great achievements. Pre-Socratic speculation would no longer strike us as rudimentary and infantile, but as the crowning epoch in a development covering many more ages than history can record.

I have spoken of this epoch as the discovery of Nature—a phrase which calls for explanation.

I mean the discovery that the whole of the surrounding world of which our senses give us any knowledge is natural, not partly natural and partly supernatural. Science begins when it is understood that the universe is a natural whole, with unchanging ways of its own—ways that may be ascertainable by human reason, but are beyond the control of human action. To reach that point of view was a great achievement. If we would measure its magnitude, we must take a backward glance at certain features of the pre-scientific age. These are: (1) the detachment of the self from the external object—the discovery of the object; (2) the preoccupation of intelligence with the practical needs of action in dealing with the object; (3) the belief in unseen, supernatural powers, behind or within the object to be dealt with.

(1) With regard to the first point—the detachment of the self from the object—if it is true that the individual still recapitulates in miniature the history of the race, we are here concerned with something that goes very far back in human development. It is only in the first weeks of life that the human baby is a solipsist, taking for granted that his environment is a part of himself. This infantile philosophy is soon disturbed by doubt. Something goes wrong: the food

supply fails to appear in immediate response to hunger. The infant cries out in anger and distress. He has to exert himself to make the environment behave as he wants. The solipsistic dream is soon shattered. In a month or so, he will be aware that there are other things, outside himself, to be cajoled or circumvented. The baby (as nurses say) 'begins to take notice', or (as Virgil says) to 'recognise his mother with a smile'. The rift has begun to open between the self and the external world.

This nascent belief in the independent existence of external objects is the foundation of the philosophy of common sense, forced on the infant by the breakdown of his naïve solipsism. In the development of the race, the discovery that there are things outside the self must, as I said, lie very far back. But it is one thing to make this discovery, and quite another to reach the idea that these external objects have a nature of their own, foreign to man's nature, and having neither sympathy nor hostility towards his passions and desires. A very long time must elapse before the line between the self and the object will be drawn where science draws it, and the object will be completely detached.

(2) The reason is that the intelligence remains, for all this long period, immersed in the interests

of action, and has no leisure for disinterested speculation. That is the second feature of the pre-scientific age. In man, as in the higher animals, the primary use of intelligence was to devise means to compassing practical ends that cannot be immediately achieved. If you offer a banana to an ape, the ape will take it and begin to eat; there is no call for reflection. But if you hang the banana out of reach, action is held up. Intelligence must be summoned to the aid of thwarted desire. There is a pause before action can be resumed. When we have observed the action that follows we fill in that pause with a rudimentary train of reasoning. We imagine that the ape has reflected: 'How can I get that banana? Here are some boxes. If I pile them up and climb on them, I shall be able to reach it'. What really happened in the ape's mind we cannot know. But we do know that man has used intelligence to overcome unusual obstacles to action, and, by the invention of tools and implements of all sorts, has extended his natural powers by natural means, and is still extending them. Thus intelligence at all times serves the purposes of action; and we conjecture that at first it served those purposes exclusively.

The limitation of the intelligence to things that merit attention because they can be turned to some practical purpose is still characteristic of savages. Dr Malinowski[1] writes about the Melanesian:

The outer world interests him in so far as it yields things useful. Utility here of course must be understood in its broadest sense, including not only what man can consume as food, use for shelter and implement, but all that stimulates his activities in play, ritual, war, or artistic production.

All such significant things stand out for the savage as isolated, detached units against an undifferentiated background. When moving with savages through any natural milieu—sailing on the sea, walking on a beach or through the jungle, or glancing across the starlit sky—I was often impressed by their tendency to isolate the few objects important to them, and to treat the rest as mere background. In a forest a plant or tree would strike me, but on inquiry I would be informed—'Oh, that is just "bush"'. An insect or bird which plays no part in the tradition or the larder would be dismissed ' Mauna wala'—'merely a flying animal'. But if, on the contrary, the object happened to be useful in one way or another, it would be named; detailed reference to its uses and properties would be given, and the thing thus would be distinctly individualised....Everywhere there is the tendency to isolate that which stands in some connection, tradi-

[1] C. K. Ogden and I. A. Richards, *The Meaning of Meaning* (1930), Supplement I, p. 331.

tional, ritual, useful to man, and to bundle all the rest into one indiscriminate heap.

(3) At first, then, the scope of thought was bounded by the imperious needs of action. External things were selected for notice in proportion as they entered into human activities. They were not interesting for what they are in themselves, but as things we can do something with, or that can act upon us. Let us now consider them in this second capacity, as agents.

To go back to our ape, pausing in his thwarted desire to seize the banana. In the interval of suspended action, we may imagine him feeling that things are opposing his desire with some contrary will of their own—an experience familiar enough in his dealings with his brother apes. There are resistances to be overcome—powers to be circumvented by his own power. And when he perceives that the boxes will help him to gain his end, he will feel that the world is not all against him: there are also things with benevolent intentions that sympathise with and forward his wishes. These helpful or harmful intentions, these unseen forces that further or thwart action, are fragmentary elements of personality. They are the raw material from which man, when he began to reflect, constructed the supernatural world. In Roman religion we find countless *numina*—

powers whose whole content is expressed in abstract nouns, *nomina*: Janua is not a fully personal god presiding over doorways, but simply the spirit of 'doorness', conceived as a power present in all doors, that can help or harm one who passes through them. From such elementary *numina* there is a scale ranging through spirits of various kinds up to the completely anthropomorphic god, like the gods of Homer.

These fragmentary elements of personality at first simply reside in things. In a sense, they are projected from man's self into the object; but we must not think of them as the creations of any conscious theory. In a census return, primitive man would not have entered his religion as 'Animist', or even as 'Pre-animist'. The assumption that helpful or harmful things have the will to help or harm is made as unreflectingly as by the child who kicks a door that has pinched his finger, or by the man who curses his golf club for slicing a stroke. If such a man were logical, he would pray to his golf clubs before beginning a match; or he would murmur some spell to charm them into hitting straight. For these projected elements of personality are the proper objects of magical art. They are 'supernatural', in that their behaviour is not regular and calculable; you cannot be sure which way they will act, as you can be sure that if you touch flame you will be burnt. Magic includes a whole collection of practices designed to bring these supernatural forces under some measure of control. And if they are to be controlled, the more we can know of their nature and habits the better. Mythology supplies this need by fabricating a history of the supernatural, with the effect of fixing the unseen powers in more definite shape and endowing them with more concrete substance. They become detached from the things in which at first they resided, and are filled out into complete persons. So magic and mythology occupy the immense outer region of the unknown, encompassing the small field of matter-of-fact ordinary knowledge. The supernatural lies everywhere within or beyond the natural; and the knowledge of the supernatural which man believes himself to possess, not being drawn from ordinary direct experience, seems to be knowledge of a different and higher order. It is a revelation, accessible only to the inspired or (as the Greeks said) 'divine' man—the magician and the priest, the poet and the seer.

Now the birth of science in Greece is marked by the tacit denial of this distinction between two orders of knowledge, experience and revelation, and between the two corresponding orders of existence, the natural and the supernatural. The Ionian cosmogonists assume (without even feeling the need to make the assertion) that the whole universe is natural, and potentially within the reach of knowledge as ordinary and rational as our knowledge that fire burns and water drowns. That is what I meant by the discovery of Nature. The conception of Nature is extended to incorporate what had been the domain of the supernatural. The supernatural, as fashioned by mythology, simply disappears; all that really exists is natural.

Enough, perhaps, has been said to justify the statement that the discovery of Nature was one of the greatest achievements of the human mind. Like all other great achievements, it was the work of a very few individuals with exceptional gifts. Why were these individuals Ionian Greeks of the sixth century?

The Ionian cities in Asia Minor were then at the height of Western civilisation. There were men in them who had outgrown the magical practices that were never to die out among the peasantry. They had also outgrown the Olympian religion of Homer. Thanks to the poets, the anthropomorphic tendency of myth had overreached itself. The Greek imagination was, perhaps, unique in visual clarity, far surpassing the

Roman in this respect. The supernatural powers had taken human shapes so concrete and well defined that a Greek could recognise any god by sight. When the tall and bearded Barnabas and the restless eloquent Paul came to Lystra, the inhabitants at once identified them as Zeus and Hermes. It was inevitable that, when the gods had become completely human persons, some sceptical mind should refuse to believe that a thunderstorm in Asia Minor was really due to the anger of a deity seated on the summit of Olympus. In the sixth century Xenophanes attacked anthropomorphic polytheism with devastating finality:

If horses or oxen had hands and could draw or make statues, horses would represent the forms of the gods like horses, oxen like oxen.

Henceforth natural science annexed to its province all that went on 'aloft' in the sky or 'under the earth'. Thunder and lightning, Anaximander said, were caused by the blast of the wind. Shut up in a thick cloud, the wind bursts forth, and then the tearing of the cloud makes the noise, and the rift gives the appearance of a flash in contrast with the blackness of the cloud. This is a typically scientific 'explanation'. There is no longer a supernatural background, peopled with fragmentary or complete personalities accessible to prayer and sacrifice or amenable to magical compulsion. Intelligence is cut off from action. Thought is left confronting Nature, an impersonal world of things, indifferent to man's desires and existing in and for themselves. The detachment of self from the object is now complete.

To the few advanced intellects who had reached this point of view, it probably seemed that they had disposed of mythology, once for all, as simply false. It is important to bear in mind that they did not carry with them the rest of the Greek world. For a thousand years the smoke of sacrifice was still to rise from the altars of Zeus. Minds not less acute and possibly more profound felt that myth was not a baseless figment of superstition, but was like the Muses of Hesiod, who knew not only how to speak falsehood in the guise of truth, but also, when they would, how to utter the truth itself. The Aphrodite and Artemis of the *Hippolytus* and the Dionysus of the *Bacchae* were to Euripides something more than either projections of human psychology or fictitious personifications of natural forces. So myth was destined to survive the contempt of Ionian rationalism and to await reinterpretation.

But at the moment we are now considering science seems to have swept mythology away.

The systems of the sixth century are cast in the form of cosmogony. Two principal questions are answered. First, how did the world we see come to be arranged as it is: at the centre, the earth with the great masses of water in the hollow seas; round it the airy region of mist and cloud and rain; and beyond that the heavenly fires? Secondly, how did life arise within this order? The answer is a history of the birth of a world order out of an initial state of things (a 'beginning', *arché*).

Take for illustration the most complete and daring of these cosmogonies, the system of Thales' successor, Anaximander, which set the pattern for the Ionian tradition. At first there was an unbounded and unordered mass of indiscriminate stuff, containing the antagonistic powers of heat and cold. This mass had the living property of eternal motion. At some point a nucleus, pregnant with these warring powers, took shape—a rationalised equivalent of the world-egg of mythical cosmogony. Perhaps because the hostility of the hot and the cold drove them apart, the nucleus was differentiated. The cold became a watery mass of earth enveloped in cloud; the hot, a sphere of flame enwrapping the whole, like bark round a tree. Then the sphere of flame burst, and was torn off to form rings of fire enclosed and hidden in dark mist. Sun, moon and stars, the points of light we see in the sky, are spouts of fire issuing from holes in these opaque rings, as the air issues from the nozzle of a bellows. The earth was then dried by the heat of the heavenly fires, and the seas shrank into their hollow beds. At last, life arose in the warm slime. The first animals were like sea-urchins enclosed in prickly shells. From these sea creatures, land animals, including man, were evolved.

The significance of this cosmogony lies not so much in what it contains as in what it leaves out. Cosmogony has been detached from theogony. There is not a word about the gods or any supernatural agency. This new form of thought brings into the field of everyday experience what had previously lain outside that field. We may see the difference by contrasting this history of the world with the old poetical theogony of Hesiod. As Hesiod looked back in time from his own age and the life he knew and dealt with every day, past the earlier ages—the Heroic Age, the Silver Age—to the dominion of Cronos and the elder gods, and beyond that to the birth of the gods themselves from the mysterious marriage of Heaven and Earth, it must have seemed that the world became less and less like the common world of familiar experience. The events —the marriage and birth of the gods, the war of the Olympians and the Titans, the legend of Prometheus—were not events of the same order as what happened in Boeotia in Hesiod's time. We may get the same impression by thinking of the Book of Genesis—all the events from creation down to the call of Abraham. As we follow the story we gradually emerge into the world we know, and the superhuman figures dwindle down to human proportions. That is how the past had looked to everyone before the rise of Ionian science. It was an extraordinary feat of rational thinking, to dissipate this haze of myth from the origins of the world and of life. Anaximander's system pushes back to the very beginning the operation of ordinary forces such as we see at work in Nature every day. The formation of the world becomes a natural, not a supernatural, event.

Such were the Ionian cosmogonies of the sixth century: they told how an ordered world was evolved out of an undifferentiated initial state of things. In the fifth century, science takes a somewhat different line, which it has followed ever since. Retaining the form of cosmogony, it becomes more particularly an inquiry into the ultimate constitution of material substance—the uniform and permanent 'nature of things'. Let us consider, in conclusion, the outcome of this inquiry—the Atomism of Democritus.

Atomism is a theory of the nature of tangible bodily substance. The notion of substance is taken from common sense. The belief in substantial things outside ourselves goes back to the original detachment of self from the object. A substance is something that exists independently of my seeing or touching it—something that endures, as the same thing, whether I am there to see it or not. The problem for science is: What is this substance that endures when it has ceased to yield us sensations? I have under my eyes what I call a sheet of paper. What I actually see is a white area with black marks. When I touch it, I feel the resistance of a smooth surface, and I can trace with my finger its rectangular shape. These sensations are my only assurance that something is there, outside me. If I turn my eyes in another direction, the whiteness and the black marks disappear. I have only the tactile sensations of the resistance of the smooth rectangular surface. If I lift my finger, these sensations also disappear. Yet I am absolutely certain that something is still there—a substance which does not depend upon my having sensations derived from it. Which of these properties—white and black, resistance, smoothness, shape—really belong independently to the thing outside me, and continue to exist when I am not looking and touching?

The Atomists held that the tactile properties are the real ones; the visual properties are not substantial or objective. They are not there when I am not looking. In a dark room the sheet of paper would lose its colour; I should see nothing. But I should still feel the shape and resistance of the surface. If I could not detect those properties, I should feel nothing and be sure the thing was not there. If I did detect them, I should be certain that, when I turned on the light, the visual properties would spring into existence again.

By this train of thought common sense can be led towards the fundamental doctrines of Atomism. The atoms of Democritus are hard bodies, too small to be seen, and deprived of all properties except shape and resistance—the tangible properties necessary and sufficient to convince us that something real is there. A larger body is not destroyed when it is broken up into atoms. All the pieces are still there, and they can be reassembled. Also they can move in space without suffering any change of quality. Atomism held that the real—the enduring and unchanging core of substance—is nothing but atoms, moving in empty space. Not only are these atoms real, but they are the whole of reality.

I do not mean to suggest that the Atomism of Democritus was actually reached by the train of thought I have outlined. In historical fact, it arose as a mathematical theory that matter consists of discrete units. But the result is the same. The atoms of Democritus are tiny bodies, into which larger bodies can be cut up, but which cannot themselves be cut into smaller pieces. They are absolutely solid, compact, impenetrable.

Where scientific Atomism went beyond common sense was in its demand that the atoms of body shall be absolutely indestructible and unchanging. This was a requirement of the reason. Common sense, untutored by science, would suppose that bodies can be, and constantly are being, destroyed. A thing will remain the same thing for a time, though some of its properties change; but then it may simply cease to exist and something else will come into being. But ancient science, holding to the principle that nothing can come out of nothing, demanded some permanent and indestructible 'being' behind the screen of shifting appearances. This postulate met the same rational need that has prompted the assertion by modern science of the principle of conservation in various forms: the law of inertia, the conservation of mass, the conservation of energy. It has been observed that all these propositions were at first announced either without proof of any sort or as the result of *a priori* demonstration, although later they have often been regarded as purely empirical laws.[1] The something—whatever it may be—of which modern science has required the conservation corresponds to the permanent 'being' or 'nature of things' required by the ancients. For the Atomists it was impenetrable particles of material substance.

Ancient science, having deduced the indestructible atom, thought it had arrived at the real nature of things. The variable qualities which things seem to have, but atoms have not—colours, tastes, and so forth—were disposed of as mere sensations which fall inside our organs of perception. They are not 'substantial', for they depend on us for their existence. Atoms alone are real, with the void in which they move and strike one another.

The essential feature of this Atomism is that it is a materialist doctrine. By that I do not mean merely that it is an account of the nature of material substance or body. It is materialist in the sense that it declares that material substance,

[1] Cf. E. Meyerson, *De l'explication dans les sciences* (Paris, 1921), ii, 327; Paul Tannery, *Pour l'histoire de la science hellène* (Paris, 1887), p. 264.

tangible body, is not only real but the whole of reality. Everything that exists or happens is to be explained in terms of these bodily factors. The world is resolved into an invisible game of billiards. The table is empty space. The balls are atoms; they collide and pass on their motion from one to another. That is all: nothing else is real. There are no players in this game. If three balls happen to make a cannon, that is a mere stroke of luck—necessary, not designed. The game consists entirely of flukes; and there is no controlling intelligence behind.

Considered as a theory of the nature of material substance, Atomism was a brilliant hypothesis. Revived by modern science, it has led to the most important discoveries in chemistry and physics. But, as I have said, ancient Atomism went farther than this. It claimed to be an account of the whole of reality—not a mere scientific hypothesis, but a complete philosophy. As such, it should include an account of the spiritual aspect of the world, as well as of the material. But when we consider the system from that standpoint, we find that anything we can recognise as spiritual has simply disappeared. When the Atomist is asked for an account of the soul, he replies that the soul (like everything else) consists of atoms. These soul-atoms are of the same impenetrable substance as all others; only they are spherical in shape, and so can move very easily and slip in between the angular and less mobile atoms of the body. Sensation is due to atoms from outside knocking up against the soul-atoms. The variety of qualities we perceive corresponds to the variety of atomic shapes. As late as 1675, a French chemist,[1] whose treatise remained classical for half a century, wrote:

The hidden nature of a thing cannot be better explained than by attributing to its parts shapes corresponding to all the effects it produces. No one will deny that the acidity of a liquid consists in pointed particles. All experience confirms this. You have only to taste it to feel a pricking of the tongue like that caused by some material cut into very fine points.

That statement might have been written by Lucretius, and (so far as it goes) it is a reasonable explanation of the mechanical cause of a certain sensation. But if I turn from the mechanical cause to the sensation itself, and then to the soul which has the sensation, and also has feelings, thoughts, and desires, I am not so easily convinced that the soul itself consists of round atoms, and that nothing really happens except collisions. It is much harder to believe that a process of

[1] Lémery, *Cours de Chymie*, quoted by E. Meyerson, *De l'explication dans les sciences* (Paris, 1921), I, 285.

thought or an emotion of anger is either totally unreal or else actually consists of a number of solid particles banging together. If man had begun by studying himself, rather than external Nature, he would never have reached so fantastic a conclusion.

Perhaps what I said earlier about the peculiar visual clarity of Greek mythology, may explain how science came at last to ignore or deny the spiritual, as distinct from the material. If the world has a spiritual aspect, man can only give an account of it in terms of his own spirit or mind. At first he projected elements of his own personality into external things. Then the Greek imagination developed these elements into the complete human personalities of anthropomorphic gods. Sooner or later the Greek intelligence was bound to discover that such gods do not exist. Thus mythology overreached itself and discredited the very existence of a spiritual world. Science drew the conclusion, not that the spiritual world had been misconceived, but that there was no such thing: nothing was real except tangible body composed of atoms. The result was a doctrine that philosophers call materialism, and religious people call atheism.

The Socratic philosophy is a reaction against this materialistic drift of physical science. In

order to rediscover the spiritual world, philosophy had to give up, for the moment, the search
after material substance in external Nature, and
turn its eyes inwards to the nature of the human
soul. This was the revolution accomplished by
Socrates, with his Delphic injunction 'Know
thyself'.

Chapter II

SOCRATES

We have considered the Ionian science of Nature —the germ from which all European science has since developed—as marking the achievement of an attitude of mind in which the object has been completely detached from the subject and can be contemplated by thought disengaged from the interests of action. The fruits of this attitude were the first systems of the world that can claim to be rational constructions of reality. We now come to the question, why they did not satisfy the expectations of Socrates. If the thought of these Ionians was genuinely philosophic, if they aimed at an entirely rational picture of the real, why did they disappoint a man whom the world has recognised as a great philosopher and who exalted the reason above all other faculties of man?

All our credible authorities—Plato, Xenophon, Aristotle—agree in asserting that Socrates, after his youthful disillusionment as to the methods and results of physical inquiry, never discussed such questions as the origin of the world. Xenophon[1] adds some reasons. Did men of

[1] *Memorabilia*, I, i, 11–16.

science imagine they understood human concerns so well that they could afford to neglect them for the study of things outside man's sphere and beyond his power of discovering the truth? They did not even agree among themselves, but contradicted one another on fundamental points. Did they hope, by studying the heavens, to control the weather; or were they content to know how the wind comes to blow and the rain to fall? Socrates himself, says Xenophon, only discussed human concerns—what makes men good as individuals or as citizens. Knowledge in this field was the condition of a free and noble character; ignorance left a man no better than a slave.

If Xenophon may be trusted, Socrates rejected the current speculation about Nature on two grounds: it was dogmatic, and it was useless.

The first is the objection of one who is asked to accept what he is confidently told by men who cannot know that what they say is true. These Ionians had described the origin of the world with as much assurance as if they had been there to witness it. One of them was sure that things were ultimately composed of four elements having the four primary qualities; another was equally sure that they were composed of innumerable atoms with no differences of quality. These accounts of the nature of things were *a priori* speculations, subject to no experimental control and incapable of proof. Hippocrates, the father of medicine, rightly protested against their being made the basis of medical treatment and over-riding clinical experience. A fabrication of the reason may be as dangerously false as a fabrication of myth-making imagination. The path of science has, in fact, been strewn with the wreckage of discarded concepts, whose adherents have clung to them with an obstinacy as blind as any theologian's. 'Concerning the gods', said Protagoras, 'I cannot know for certain whether they exist or not, nor what they arc like in form. Many things hinder certainty—the obscurity of the matter and the shortness of man's life.' Socrates would be perfectly justified in saying the same of atoms. An essential characteristic of Socrates is his clear sense of what can, and what cannot, be known, and of the danger of pretending to knowledge whose grounds have never been examined. Philosophy retains the right to ask the man of science how he came by his concepts and whether they are valid.

The other objection is that these theories are useless. Xenophon betrays that he did not understand what Socrates meant by 'useless'. It was a merit, rather than a fault, in the Ionians that they could study the heavens without hoping to

control the weather or to read the fall of king-
doms and the issues of battle in the aspect of
the stars. By 'useless' Socrates rather meant
useless for what seemed to him man's chief and
proper concern—knowledge of himself and of the
right way to live. If I cannot know the beginnings of life in the unrecorded past, I can, Socrates
thought, know the end of life here and now.

This shift from the search for beginnings to the
search for ends naturally coincides with the shift
of interest from external Nature to man. The
physical science from which Socrates turned away
was not, like modern science, an attempt to formulate laws of Nature, always with an eye to the
prediction of future events and with the incidental
gain of increased control over natural forces. It
took the form of cosmogony, that is, an inquiry
how the world came to be as it is; and, secondly,
it asked what is the ultimate nature of that
material substance of which things, now and
always, consist. The answer to these questions
seemed to lie in the past leading up to the present.
Science tried to get back to the beginning of
things or to the material principles from which
things come into being. The future held out no
promise of anything different. But as soon as we
turn to consider our own lives, our thoughts are
nearly always bent upon the future. The past

cannot be changed; and the soundest of instincts bids us keep our backs turned to it and face towards what is coming. In the future lie the ends that we desire and hope to compass by the exercise of will and choice. The future appears as a realm of contingency and freedom, not, like the past, as a closed record of unchangeable necessity.

Socrates, recounting his experiences in the passage I quoted from the *Phaedo*, tells how he caught at the suggestion that the world was the work of intelligence, and hoped to find that Anaxagoras would explain how the order of things was designed for the best. Physical speculation, he thought, could be transformed into a significant and intelligible account, if men of science would look in the other direction and consider the world, not as a realm of mechanical necessity, but as a process towards an end—an end that was good, and therefore an object of rational design. This passage contains a forecast of Plato's system of the world; but Socrates himself did not feel equal to the task of transforming the science of Nature. He only prepared the way by concentrating attention upon human life, a field in which the question of the ends we are to live for is paramount.

This question—what is the end of life?—is one that, then as now, was rarely asked. When a man becomes a doctor, he has settled that his business is to cure the sick. Thenceforward he lives mostly by routine. When he has to pause and think what to do next, he thinks about means, not about the value of the end. He does not ask: 'Ought this patient to be cured, or would it be better if he died? What is the value of health, or of life itself, in comparison with other valuable things?' Nor does the tradesman pause to ask: 'Ought I to get more money? What is the value of riches?' So we go on from day to day, contriving means to settled ends, without raising the question whether the ends are worth living for. That is precisely the question Socrates did raise, and forced others to consider, thereby causing a good deal of discomfort. Taking life as a whole, he asked which of the ends we pursue are really and intrinsically valuable, not mere means to something else we think desirable. Is there some one end of life that is alone worthy of desire?

Now it would not be hard to convince a tradesman that money is not an end in itself. He would agree that he wants money for the sake of something else that he might call pleasure or happiness. And a doctor might admit that health is valuable only as a condition of happiness. In that way human happiness emerges as a common end, to which other aims are subordinate. But

what is happiness? From Socrates' time onwards, this was the chief question debated by the
Schools. The philosophers saw that mankind
might be roughly classified under three types,
according as they identified happiness with
pleasure, with social success, honour, and fame,
or with knowledge and wisdom. The debate
turned on the relative claims of these three main
objects of pursuit. Could any one of them by
itself constitute happiness, and if so, which one?
Or were they all constituents in a perfect life;
and, if so, how were they to be related to one
another? We are now concerned with Socrates'
solution of this problem.

Socrates held that happiness was to be found
in what he called the perfection of the soul—
'making one's soul as good as possible'—and
that all other ends which men desire were strictly
of no value in themselves. If they were worth
pursuing at all, they were so only as means to the
perfection of the soul. In Plato's *Apology*, which
is no doubt faithful in spirit and substance to the
speech actually made by Socrates in his own de-
fence, Socrates refuses to accept acquittal at the
price of giving up the search after wisdom and
the mission which he describes as follows:

If you should offer to acquit me on these terms, my
answer would be: 'Athenians, I hold you in much

affection and esteem; but I will obey heaven rather than you, and, so long as breath and strength are in me, I will never cease from seeking wisdom or from exhorting you and pointing out the truth to any of you whom I may chance to meet, in my accustomed words: My good friend, you are a citizen of Athens, a great city famous for wisdom and strength; are you not ashamed to spend so much trouble upon heaping up riches and honour and reputation, while you care nothing for wisdom and truth and the perfection of your soul? And if he protests that he does care for these things, I shall not at once release him and go my way; I shall question and cross-examine and test him, and if I think he does not possess the virtue he affects, I shall reproach him for holding the most precious things cheap and worthless things dear. This I shall do to everyone whom I meet, young or old, citizen or stranger, but especially to you, my fellow-citizens, inasmuch as you are my own people. For be assured that such is heaven's command; and I believe that no better piece of fortune has ever befallen you in Athens than my enlistment in the service of heaven.

For I have no other business but to go about persuading you all, both young and old, to care less for your bodies and your wealth than for the perfection of your souls, and to make that your first concern, and telling you that goodness does not come from wealth, but it is goodness that makes wealth or anything else, in public or in private life, a thing of value for man. If by saying this I am demoralising the young men, so much the worse; but if it is asserted that I have anything else to say, then that is not true. Therefore, Athenians', I should conclude, 'you may listen to Anytus or not; you may acquit me or not; for I shall not change my ways, though I were to die a thousand deaths'.

By 'the perfection of the soul' Socrates meant, I believe, what we might call spiritual perfection. In this he saw man's proper concern; and if he put aside speculations about the origin and constitution of the world as 'useless', he meant that knowledge of these things, even if it could be gained, would not throw light on the nature of spiritual perfection or on the means of attaining to it. For that purpose knowledge of a different kind was needed—namely, a direct insight (of which every man was capable) into the value of the various things we desire. This is the knowledge which Socrates identified with goodness in the famous paradox usually translated 'Virtue is knowledge'. From another point of view, this knowledge may be called 'self-knowledge'—the recognition of that self or soul in each of us whose perfection is the true end of life. Socrates' claim to rank among the greatest philosophers rests upon his discovery of this soul and of a morality of spiritual aspiration, to take the place of the current morality of social constraint.

In order to appreciate the significance of these

discoveries, we must glance here at the movement
of thought associated with Socrates' contemporaries and rivals, the Sophists. The Sophists
were not a school; they were individual teachers
of very various types. But we find scattered
utterances of one or another Sophist, which fit
together as elements in a philosophy of life
characteristic of this period in Greek thought,
especially at Athens. We might call it, I would
suggest, the philosophy of adolescence. Let us
pursue the analogy I put forward earlier, between
the growth of early philosophic speculation and
the development of the individual mind in childhood and youth. We thought of the earliest
science of Nature as the culmination of an age-
long process. The birth of science marked the
moment when man succeeded in detaching his
own nature from the world outside. Resigning
the pathetic dream of controlling an environment
animated by powers and passions akin to his own,
he found out that he knew much less about the
world than he had imagined; and the keenest
intellects were inspired with a fresh curiosity to
penetrate the hidden reality of things in themselves. Absorbed in the interest of the object,
man forgot to think about himself. There is something in this outward-looking curiosity that re-
calls the divine wonder in the eyes of a child, when

you make the most of a little information about variable stars, or electrons, or the circulation of the blood. From this standpoint, we might regard pre-Socratic science as the childhood of the new form of thought. The sixth-century Ionians had reached a stage analogous to the attitude of a child's mind from (say) the age of six to the beginning of adolescence. In that period of our lives we have given up the solipsism of the new-born infant, and have ceased to believe that fairy tales are literally true. The normal child is then not only interested in things for practical purposes, but genuinely curious and capable of wonder about things in themselves. He has a power of enjoying knowledge for its own sake, until this enjoyment is killed by what is known as education. In the child, too, this curiosity is looking outwards, self-forgetful. Conduct offers no field for independent speculation. Life is ordered by the authority of nurses and parents; and, however much naughtiness there may be, some authority is normally accepted as infallible.

Childhood ends in the most revolutionary crisis of human life—adolescence. What I would now suggest is that adolescence corresponds to the second phase of Greek philosophy—the age of the Sophists.

During adolescence, (say) from fourteen to

twenty, the youth is engaged in a second effort of
detachment, more conscious and much more pain-
ful than the infant's detachment of the self from
the outer world. He becomes self-conscious in
a new way. It is now his central concern to detach his individual self from his parents and the
family group, and from every other social group
claiming to dominate his will and warp his personality. The individual has to find himself as a
moral being who must learn to stand upon his
own feet, as a man. That he should succeed in this
effort of detachment is of vital importance; and
it might seem that the chief end of education
should be to help him through it, with the least
damage to himself and to the society of which he
must remain a member. The education we actually
offer seems rather to run counter to this aim. The
boy is set to learn many things that might satisfy
disinterested curiosity, if curiosity had not given
place to a more urgent need; and he is surrounded
by the almost overwhelming pressure of a group
of contemporaries demanding absolute conformity to a standard that he ought to outgrow.
The result is a reaction against all authority
which is unnecessarily violent.

Now in Greek society, after the Persian wars
of the first quarter of the fifth century, we can
observe, with admirable clearness, an analogous

effort of the individual to detach himself from the
social group—the city and its traditional customs.
Until that time, the claim of authority to regulate
the citizen's conduct had not been explicitly
challenged. However much or little individual
conduct conformed in fact to the customs and
laws of society, it had been tacitly acknowledged
that those customs and laws embodied an absolute
obligation, beyond dispute. But in the time of
Socrates some of the Sophists began to cast doubt
on this basic assumption with a daring which
seemed to conservative minds to threaten the
whole structure of society.

Take, for example, a recently discovered frag-
ment of the Sophist Antiphon, which draws a
significant contrast between the laws of the state
and the law of Nature. The law of Nature is declared to be the principle of self-preservation—
that each individual should seek after what is
advantageous to life and consequently pleasant.
The laws of the state, on the other hand, enjoin
behaviour that is unpleasant and therefore un-
natural. Such laws are contrary to Nature, which
is the true standard of right. On what does their
professed authority rest? On nothing more than
convention. Legal rules were originally created
by human agreement, and they are not naturally
binding on posterity who were not parties to the

covenant. The practical conclusion is that, whereas the laws of Nature cannot be evaded, the laws of society should be obeyed only when there is a risk of being found out and punished. Nature will always find you out; but, with luck or cunning on your side, society may not.

The contrast between the law of Nature and human law appears here for the first time. It is only now that the Greek mind clearly perceives that social laws are not divine institutions operating with inevitable sanctions like the penalties of transgressing against natural law. The theory of social contract is announced. Individuals, it is alleged, were originally free to seek each man his own self-preservation, pleasure, and self-interest. For some reason, perhaps for the advantage of mutual protection against hostile groups, a number of individuals agreed to surrender their freedom. But the laws they made have no other source of obligation. The naturally strong man is like a lion entangled in a net of prohibition and constraint. He has a natural right to break loose, if he can, as Gulliver threw off the Lilliputian bonds, and go forth in his strength to claim the lion's share.[1]

[1] This view of the natural right of the stronger is stated with great force by Callicles, the young man of the world in Plato's *Gorgias*, p. 482 ff.

In this philosophy of individual self-assertion parents will recognise something analogous to the spirit of adolescent reaction against the authority of the home. It will not surprise them that the Sophists found eager listeners among the youths who attended their lectures and debates. In the Greek city there were no secondary schools. After adolescence, the state itself was regarded as the educational institution which shaped the young citizen. What it taught him was the established law, a precious legacy of ancestral, or even divine, wisdom. In this public school the only masters were the elder citizens; and in their ears such an utterance as Antiphon's was no less outrageous than it would sound to the public-school master of to-day. To the boys, on the other hand, it would come as an equally welcome expression of the rebellion against those stupid rules.

What was Socrates' attitude towards this philosophy of adolescence? In the popular mind he was simply confused with the Sophists. Aristophanes and the other comedians had fostered the misconception. At the age of seventy he was tried and condemned for 'not recognising the gods of Athens' and for 'demoralising the young men'. Were these charges entirely false, or do they represent some truth far more profound than the superficial sense they bore in the mouths of his accusers?

Socrates was ready to converse with anyone; but above all he welcomed the company of the adolescent young. They found in him exactly what youth needs in this phase of reaction—a man whose proved courage they could respect and admire, and whose subtle intellect was always at the service of the youthful passion for argument. He would never silence their crude questionings with the superior tone of adult experience; he wanted to know all that was going on in their minds, and positively encouraged them to think for themselves on every subject, and especially about right and wrong. He always said, with manifest candour, that he was himself an inquirer, who knew nothing and had nothing to teach, but regarded every question as an open question. And behind the play of humorous intelligence, they felt the presence of an extraordinary personality, calm and secure in the possession of a mysterious wisdom. Here was one who had found the secret of life, and achieved in his own character a balance and harmony which nothing could disturb. His time was always at the disposal of anyone who would set about discovering that secret for himself—above all, the youth whose obscure but pressing need was to achieve the freedom of self-ruling man-hood.

Superficial readers of the early dialogues some-times carry away the impression that Socrates laid traps for his opponents and argued for victory. Since Plato himself condemns this practice of 'Eristic'—verbal contention without regard for truth—he cannot have meant to repre-sent it as characteristic of Socrates. A careful reader will notice that Socrates plays tricks of this sort only when he is exposing the pretensions of professional rhetoricians and debaters or of others who claimed some superior wisdom. Such men cannot be brought to co-operate in the search for truth; they think they already possess the truth or something that will do as well. The wise man can only fight them with their own weapons and so convince their young admirers that verbal cleverness is not wisdom. His method in talking with young men is different. He be-gins by puzzling them in order that they may see how little they really understand, and be ready to seek the truth in his company. Once the genuine search has begun, he always treats the other party to the conversation as a companion and ally, not as an opponent.

Socrates said that he knew nothing that could be taught to anyone else. At the same time he declared that human perfection lies in the knowledge of good and evil. Why cannot this knowledge be taught, like knowledge of other kinds? Because all that another person can teach me is that such and such things are believed to be good, such and such actions are believed to be right, by some external authority or by society itself. Information of this sort can be conveyed by instruction; indeed, it forms the whole substance of moral education as commonly practised. But it is not what Socrates called knowledge. I shall not know that this or that is good or right until I can see it directly for myself; and, as soon as I can see it for myself, that knowledge will put out of court what I am told that other people believe or think they believe. Knowledge of values, in fact, is a matter of direct insight, like seeing that the sky is blue, the grass green. It does not consist of pieces of information that can be handed from one mind to another. In the last resort, every individual must see and judge for himself what it is good for him to do. The individual, if he is to be a complete man, must become morally autonomous, and take his own life into his own control.

This is a responsibility that no individual can escape. He can indeed, once for all, accept some external authority, and thenceforward treat that authority as responsible for what it tells him to do. But he remains responsible for his original choice of an authority to be obeyed. Socrates held that the judge within each of us cannot depute his functions to another. A man perfect in self-knowledge can tell when his own vision of what is good is clear; he cannot see into another's mind and tell whether *his* vision is clear.

This view presupposes that every human soul possesses the necessary power of immediate insight or perception of good and evil. As with the bodily eye, the soul's vision may be clouded and dim, and it may be deceived by false appearances. Pleasure, for instance, is constantly mistaken for good when it is not really good. But when the eye of the soul does see straight and clearly, then there is no appeal from its decision. In the field of conduct, education (after the necessary tutelage of childhood) is not teaching; it is opening the eye of the soul, and clearing its vision from the distorting mists of prejudice, and from the conceit of knowledge which is really no more than second-hand opinion.

It is not surprising that the elder citizens of Athens, when they learnt (perhaps from disagreeable encounters with their own adolescent sons) that Socrates encouraged the young to call in question every moral precept, saw no difference between his doctrine and Antiphon's and concluded that he was demoralising the young men. If we take our own word 'de-moralise' in its literal sense, the charge was true. To tell the young that, in order to gain the full freedom of manhood, they must question every received maxim of conduct and aim at judging every moral question for themselves, is to demoralise them in the sense of cutting away every moral prop and buttress with which parents and society have so studiously environed their childhood. Socrates was, in fact, undermining the morality of social constraint—that morality of obedience to authority and of conformity to custom, which has held together human groups of whatever size, from the family to the nation, throughout the whole history of the race. Or rather, he was going beyond this morality of constraint and prohibition to a morality of a different type, in the same way that the Sermon on the Mount goes beyond the law delivered on Sinai. The spring of this new morality lies within the soul itself. It may be called the morality of aspiration to spiritual perfection. If spiritual perfection be taken as the end of life and the secret of happiness, and if every human soul can see its own good, then action cannot be governed by any code of rules imposed from without. Whether such rules are valid in any actual case is a question that can be decided only by the sincere and dispassionate verdict of the individual soul.

To discover a new principle of morality, and to proclaim it without fear or compromise, is to incur the resentment of society living by the morality whose limitations are to be broken down. It is also to incur the risk of being misunderstood by hearers who are already chafing at those limits, but may not be capable of grasping the new principle in its positive implications. Certainly it is dangerous to say: 'Do that which is right in your own eyes', because some of your hearers will run away with the notion that you mean: 'Do just as you please'; and will not grasp the all-important proviso: 'But first make sure that your eyes see with perfect clearness what is really good'. If that condition is satisfied, if you see the truth and act upon it—as you must, when you really see it—you will find happiness in possessing your own soul; but you may find that doing what you know to be right may be anything but pleasant; it may cost you poverty and suffering and, if you cannot avoid a conflict with society, imprisonment and death. If the condition is not satisfied, you may become a self-seeking sensualist and, if your egoism is allied with power, an enemy of mankind, a wolf whom society has every right to destroy. Then you will have lost your own soul and not found happiness, though you may have reached the heights of power which the world thinks most enviable.

I can now define more clearly what I meant by saying that the achievement of Socrates was the discovery of the soul. When he told the Athenians that the only thing in life worth caring for was not wealth or social distinction, but the soul, he was using language which sounded very strange to their ears.[1] The ordinary Athenian thought of his soul—his psyche—as an airy unsubstantial wraith or double of his body, a shadow that, at the moment of death, might flit away to some dismal Hades bordering on nonexistence, or perhaps escape as a breath to be dissipated like smoke in the air. If he spoke of his 'self', he meant his body, the warm and living seat of consciousness—a consciousness that was doomed to fade with the waning faculties of age and to perish with the body at death. To tell him that his chief concern was to care for his 'soul' and its perfection, was like telling him to neglect his substance and cherish his shadow.

Socrates' discovery was that the true self is not the body but the soul. And by the soul he

[1] Cf. J. Burnet, *The Socratic doctrine of the Soul*, Essays and Addresses (1929), p. 126.

meant the seat of that faculty of insight which can know good from evil and infallibly choose the good. Self-knowledge implies the recognition of this true self. Self-examination is a discipline constantly needed to distinguish its judgment from the promptings of other elements in our nature, closely attached to the body and its distracting interests. Self-rule is the rule of the true self over those other elements—an absolute autocracy of the soul. For this inner judge of good and evil is also a ruler. The true self is a faculty, not only of intuitive insight, but of will— a will that can override all other desires for pleasure and seeming happiness. The soul which sees what is really good infallibly desires the good it has discerned. Socrates held that this desire of the enlightened soul is so strong that it cannot fail to overpower all the other desires whose objects the true self sees to be illusory.

This is the meaning of the Socratic paradoxes: 'Virtue is knowledge', 'No one does wrong wittingly'. People commonly say: 'I knew it was wrong, but I couldn't help doing it'. Socrates replies: That is never really the truth. You may have known that other people think what you did was bad, or that you had been told it was bad; but if you had known for yourself it was bad, you would not have done it. Your fault was a failure of insight. You did not see the good; you were misled by some pleasure which seemed good at the moment. If you had seen the good you would also have willed it, and acted accordingly. No one does wrong against his true will, when once that will has been directed to its object, the good, by a genuine and clear vision.

The special name given to the true self in the later writings of Plato and in Aristotle is *nous*, a word commonly translated by 'reason'. To modern ears 'spirit' is a less misleading term, because 'reason' suggests a faculty that thinks but does not also will. Plato and Aristotle regard this spirit as distinct from the *psyche*, which is inseparably associated with the body and perishes with the death of the body. For the perfection of the spirit the Greeks used the ordinary word for 'goodness', *areté*, and this had better not be translated by 'virtue'. 'Virtue', at all times, means conformity to current ideals of conduct. The virtuous man is he who does what the rest of society approves. The Socratic philosophy dismisses this conformity under the name of 'popular virtue'. Plato puts the virtue of 'the respectable citizen' on the same level with the unremitting pursuit of duty characteristic of bees, ants, and other social insects. This is not what Socrates meant by 'goodness'. The whole content of his mission was to supersede the childish morality of blameless conformity by an ideal of spiritual manhood rising above the commonly acknowledged bounds of human capacity. This was to substitute for a morality of attainable virtue, such as the world respects and rewards, a morality aspiring to a perfection unattainable save by a few men whom the world has rejected while they lived, and only learnt too late to worship as heroic or divine. Such a man was Socrates.

Chapter III

PLATO

Socrates was one of that small number of adventurers who, from time to time, have enlarged the horizon of the human spirit. They have divined in our nature unsuspected powers which only they have as yet, in their own persons, brought to fulfilment. By living the truth they discovered they gave the world the only possible assurance that it is not an illusion. By definition, it is a truth beyond the comprehension of their contemporaries and countrymen. Conviction is slowly carried to posterity by the example of their lives, not by any record they bequeath in writing. For, with a few exceptions, they have not written books. They were wise, and knew that the letter is destined to kill much (though not all) of the life that the spirit has given. The only language they could use was inevitably open to misconstruction. A new range of truth can hardly be disclosed in words bearing the worn impress of familiar usage. Those who, by intimate contact, felt the force of their personality, have believed in them, more than in anything they said.

Only by a rare stroke of fortune has one or

another of these pioneers of thought found a single disciple who could grasp his meaning well enough to perform the task of handing it on. Even so, there arises a curious dilemma, which can hardly be escaped. Unless this disciple is himself a man of genius, he is not likely to rise to the height of his argument. If he is a man of genius, he will not stop short at a mere reproduction of what he has understood from his master. He will carry the thought farther, following out its implications in fields beyond its original scope; and in so doing he may transform the truth into a shape the master would hardly recognise.

Something of this sort happened in the case of Socrates and Plato. It was the unique good fortune of Socrates to have, among his young companions, one who was not only to become a writer of incomparable skill, but was, by native gift, a poet and a thinker no less subtle than Socrates himself. Plato was about twenty-eight when Socrates died, and he went on writing till his own death at the age of eighty. A philosopher of his calibre could not limit himself to reproducing the thought of any master, however great. True, the central germ of Platonism, from first to last, is the new Socratic morality of spiritual aspiration; but under Plato's hands this germ has grown into a tree whose branches cover the heavens. Platonism is, what the doctrine of Socrates never was, a system of the world, embracing that whole province of external Nature from which Socrates had turned away to study the nature and the end of man.

The relation of Platonism to Socrates' philosophy—the question where (so to say) Socrates ends and Plato begins—is still a matter of debate among scholars. I cannot here go into this controversy. I can only describe the relation as I see it, and very much as it has been seen for a good many years past by the majority of competent judges.

We should not think of the young Plato as a cloistered student of philosophy. It must not be forgotten that, throughout his childhood and youth, Greek society was rent into two camps, which carried on for thirty years an internecine war of the kind that exhausts and demoralises both parties. We who have taken part in a similar conflict know, to our cost, how the recrudescence of physical violence lets loose the basest and cruellest passions, and transfigures into patriotic virtue impulses which in times of peace are repressed as criminal. No society can endure the moral wounds inflicted in such a struggle, lasting through a whole generation, and emerge unscathed. Anyone who has read the famous chapters in which Thucydides[1] analyses the dissolution and collapse of all moral standards in times of war and revolution, is not likely to forget them. These chapters find an echo in one of Plato's letters, where, as an old man, he looks back to the Athens of his youth and the Peloponnesian War. He speaks of his city in those days as no longer governed by the manners and institutions of his forefathers; he had seen the whole fabric of law and custom going to pieces at an alarming rate. In normal times his distinguished birth and far more distinguished gifts would have marked him out for a leading part in public life. As soon as he was of age, his influential relatives and friends were urging him to join their faction. His own ambitious inclinations tempted him to accept these flattering approaches. But he mentions two decisive events that caused him to draw back in horror and disgust. In both Socrates was involved. One was an attempt made by the leaders of the oligarchic party, the Thirty Tyrants (as they were called) —among them was Plato's uncle, Critias—to compromise Socrates by ordering him to take part in the illegal arrest of a fellow-citizen. Socrates refused, and escaped their vengeance only by the accident of their sudden fall from

[1] Book iii, ch. 82–84.

power. The other was the trial and death of
Socrates on a charge which Plato describes as
false and infamous. This judicial crime marred
the triumph of the opposite faction, the restored
democracy. These two incidents stood out in
Plato's memory as having barred for him the
avenue to political action in a society whose
rulers were capable of such evil deeds. Mean-
while, he adds, he was all the time thinking how
the moral life of Athens might be restored upon a
new foundation. The answer he found was that
the race of man could never find rest from evils
until the lovers of wisdom should become kings,
or kings, by some divine appointment, become
lovers of wisdom. This was to be the central
thesis of his central work, the *Republic*, which
contains the programme for the radical reform of
the city-state on principles deduced from the
philosophy of Socrates.

The *Republic*, however, is a mature work of his
middle life. It could not be written until Plato
had read the secret of Socrates' inmost thought
and formulated its essential significance. This
preliminary task is accomplished in the early
group of dialogues, centred round the *Apology*.[1]

[1] The most important works in this early group
are: *The Apology, Crito, Euthyphro, Laches, Charmides,
Lysis, Protagoras, Gorgias.*

The *Apology* itself is a document of unique authority. It is the only direct statement of the
meaning of Socrates' life written by a man capable of penetrating to that meaning. The dialogues
belonging to the same group give dramatic
pictures of Socrates actually at work, partly for
the purpose of defending his memory, but still
more for Plato's other purpose of discovering,
for himself and for the world, the gist and outcome of his master's thought. The account I have
given of Socrates' doctrine is based upon the
results which Plato alone was able to formulate.
The Socrates of Xenophon is a figure that would
bulk in human history on about the same scale
as Dr Johnson. The Socrates of Plato is the real
Socrates, a figure that inspired every noble character of Greek and Roman antiquity to the last
hour of its decline.

In the dialogues of the early group we can
make out Socrates' contribution to the theory of
Forms (or 'Ideas') which is characteristic of
Platonism. The morality of aspiration, instituted
by Socrates, implies a constant effort of the soul
towards an ideal of perfection. The first condition
of any progress is that the goal should be clearly
seen and distinguished from the false lights of
Pleasure, whom Plato compares to the phantom
Helen fashioned by the gods to lure the Greeks

to Troy, when all the while the true Helen had been rapt away to Egypt. The clear vision of the ideal is knowledge, to be won only by hard thinking. In Socrates' practice, this hard thinking took the form of attempts to define the essential meaning of the terms commonly used to describe right conduct. All agree that there is such a thing as Justice, for example. What do we mean by that name? If we consider and compare the actions pronounced to be 'just' or 'right' by different people and different communities, we shall find a confused and baffling conflict of opinions. The customs thought right in one country are condemned in another country as wrong. One who lives by the old morality of social constraint, will say that his local custom is right for him, a different custom right for his neighbours. But the new morality of aspiration is universal. There can be only one ideal of perfection common to all humanity, one standard by which all customs and actions must be measured. It follows (so Plato inferred) that such a term as 'Justice' has a universal meaning, independent of all the various things that are called just at various times and places. This absolute meaning can be defined and known. It is what Plato called a 'Form' or 'ideal', fixed in the nature of things, unchangeable, beyond the reach of the

arbitrary enactments of any group or individual.

When we speak of Justice as an 'ideal', we
also mean that it may never yet have been completely embodied in any man or in any system of
institutions. It is not a mere 'idea', in the sense
of a thought or notion in our minds; for the
notions in our minds are confused and con-
flicting. They are only dim and inadequate appre-
hensions of what Justice is in itself. Justice in
itself is not a thought, but an eternal object of
thought. These names we give to the actions and
institutions we approve belong really to elements in an absolute ideal of human perfection,
an end to which all humanity must aspire, a
pattern in the heavens that has seldom been
realised on earth. Here, then—in the knowledge
and acceptance of this ideal—is the unshakable
foundation upon which a reformed society must
be built. To seek this knowledge, and be willing
to accept it, is to be a lover of wisdom; to possess
it (if man can ever possess it) is to be wise.
Hence Plato declares that the race of man will
never find rest until the lovers of wisdom become
kings. The ideal commonwealth must be ruled by
those few who have come nearest to spiritual
perfection because they know what spiritual
perfection is. Thus far Plato's characteristic

theory grows naturally out of the practice of Socrates.

The next epoch of Plato's life, about his fortieth year, is marked by his visit to the western half of the Greek world—the brilliant and luxurious cities of Southern Italy and Sicily. Here he came, for the first time, in personal contact with the Pythagorean communities, which, for a century and a half, had guarded and developed a philosophic tradition very different from the Ionian science of Nature. The Pythagorean philosophy was mathematical, but its inspiration was mystical and religious. The ancients recognised it as an independent tradition, off the main track of Ionian science. They called it the Italian philosophy because the chief Pythagorean societies were established in Lower Italy. Pythagoras himself had been another of those pioneers of thought who have bequeathed, not written doctrines, but the inspiration of a great personality. He had not, like Socrates, the good fortune to find one disciple who could interpret that inspiration; but he founded a brotherhood with a common life dedicated to the continuation of his work.

From this quarter a fresh stream flowed into the current of Plato's thought. Pythagorean influence is everywhere traceable in the dialogues of the middle period, centred round the *Republic* —the *Meno*, *Phaedo*, *Symposium*, and *Phaedrus*. The earliest signs of it are in the *Gorgias*, written probably about the time of Plato's first visit to the West. A doctrine is now announced, which (as I believe) goes beyond Socrates and is distinctively Platonic. The absolute Forms are given a substantial reality, separate from the things that embody them in our world; and at the same time the soul or spirit which knows the Forms is given a separate existence, independent of the body it inhabits for a time. Platonism proper dates, in fact, from the confluence of those two streams of inspiration—the Socratic and the Pythagorean. From Socrates Plato learnt that the problems of human life were to be solved by the morality of aspiration and the pursuit of an invariable ideal of perfection. From Pythagoras he learnt how this conception could be extended beyond the field of human concerns into a system embracing the whole of Nature and transforming the scope of science as the Socrates of the *Phaedo* wished to see it transformed. Unlike that Ionian materialism we considered at the outset, Platonism seeks the key to Nature, not in the beginning, but in the end—not in mechanical causes impelling from behind, but in final causes which attract (as it were from in front) a move-

ment of desire towards a pattern of ideal perfection.

To call this perfection 'ideal' does indeed
imply that it is not (as we say) 'realised' here,
not completely reproduced or embodied in the
world of existence in time and space. But this
does not mean that, in itself, it is unreal or
imaginary. On the contrary, the world of perfect
Forms contains all that is truly real. Reality
cannot be denied to objects that are eternal and
unchangeable and can be known by the soul.
These Forms possess the marks held to be characteristic of substance. Substantiality is to be
sought in this quarter, not where Ionian science
looked for it—in the dark and fluctuating abyss
of matter. The unchanging world of Forms
governs the flow of becoming in time and space,
as the moon governs, by her attraction, the restless tides of the sea.

Thus Platonism is a system which extends to
the interpretation of all existence the principle
of aspiration announced in the morality of
Socrates. The same (as we shall see) may be
said of the system of Aristotle, in so far as he
remains a Platonist. Accordingly these are the
two systems of Greek origin that were to prove
capable of fusion into the structure of Christian
thought, when the morality of aspiration had

been stated, once again, in a different form. Plato and Aristotle are among the greatest fathers of the Christian church. In spite of certain heretical doctrines, they might have been canonised in the Middle Ages, had they not happened to be born some centuries before the Christian era. Behind them both is Socrates, who perhaps would have waited longer, to take his place in the company of the Saints with Joan of Arc. Pythagoras also would have a strong claim; for he furnished the clue which led Plato to expand Socrates' principle of aspiration into a system of the universe.

Pythagoras is sometimes described in histories of philosophy as a man who had two separate interests—a religious reformer, who taught the doctrine of transmigration and instituted a cult society, and a man of science who did much to lay the foundations of mathematics, that is to say of arithmetic, geometry, astronomy, and music. Transmigration was, until very recent times, regarded by most modern Europeans as a rather crude and barbaric form of the doctrine of immortality. Also, it is not at once obvious to our minds that there is any connection between the immortality of the soul and mathematics. So the historian was disposed to dismiss the religious Pythagoras with brief and apologetic notice, and to concentrate on the scientific Pytha-

goras and his mathematical doctrine that the
essential reality of things is to be found in
numbers. But that is not the way to understand
a great philosopher's apprehension of the world.
The vision of philosophic genius is a unitary
vision. Such a man does not keep his thought in
two separate compartments, one for weekdays,
the other for Sundays. We begin to understand
Pythagoras when we see that the two sides of his
philosophy meet in the conception of harmony—
a conception that has a meaning both in the
spiritual and in the physical world. Let us approach it from the physical side.

The germ of this mathematical philosophy was
a discovery in the field, not of arithmetic or
geometry, but of music. Pythagoras found out
that the perfect consonances (as they are still
called) of the musical scale—the intervals of the
fourth, the fifth, and the octave—can be exactly
expressed as ratios between the numbers 1, 2, 3
and 4, which, added together, make the perfect
number, 10. The ratio of the octave is 2 : 1; the
ratio of the fifth is 3 : 2; the ratio of the fourth is
4 : 3. This discovery was, no doubt, made by
measuring, on a monochord with a movable
bridge, the lengths of string required to yield
the several notes forming the perfect intervals.[1]

---

[1] Musicians will find further details in J. Burnet,
Greek Philosophy, Part I (London, 1914), p. 46.

A practical musician might have taken it as a pleasing curiosity; but he would have continued (as the musician always has) to tune his strings by ear. An ordinary man of science might have gone on to consider what are the phenomena measured by these ratios; and he might have found out—what a later Pythagorean did find out —that they are vibrations. Pythagoras, the man of genius, divined in his discovery a principle illuminating the whole economy of Nature.

If you run your finger up or down the string of a violin, it will yield a continuous range of rising or falling sound, extending vaguely in both directions. If you stop the string at the right points, determined by these numerical ratios, it will yield a concord of sounds, the structure of a limited and harmonious order. That structure, constant through all the variety of musical scales, is the key to the whole architecture of music, opening a world not only of order but of beauty, a cosmos. In Greek 'cosmos' means beauty as well as order, and Pythagoras is said to have been the first to call the universe a cosmos. For if the chaotic welter of sounds that besiege our hearing can be reduced, by the simple principle of limiting measure, to the harmonious order of art and finally to proportions of number, might not the whole order of Nature, with its acknowledged beauty, be framed on a principle analogous or even identical? If this thought is pursued in the physical direction, it leads to the Pythagorean doctrine that the reality of things lies, not in the unordered and indefinite principle of matter (the Unlimited), but in the opposite limiting principle of form and measure, proportion and number. All things we see and touch represent or embody number. Under this aspect of measurable quantity, the world of Nature can be known and understood. In astronomy, the speeds and distances of the heavenly bodies are ruled by the proportions of a harmony that was to be known later as the harmony of the spheres. The forms or surfaces which limit tangible bodies represent the perfect figures of geometry; and the laws of these figures can be finally reduced to relations of number. This discovery—that the key to physical science lies in mathematics—is one of those intuitions of genius which date from the childhood of philosophic speculation and still serve as guiding principles to science. The physicists of this generation tell us that the laws of material substance are to be expressed in mathematical equations.

Next, turning from the macrocosm of Nature to the microcosm of man's soul and body, Pythagoras saw that the perfection of the body—its

beauty, strength, and health—depends upon a
harmony of material elements; and from his time
onwards the theory and practice of Greek medicine
were in large part governed by the principle that
healing is the restoration of a balance or proportion dislocated by disease. The same principle
was applied to the goodness or 'virtue' of the
soul, whose health is disordered by vices of excess
and defect. The perfecting of the soul is the restoration of harmony in the human cosmos. The
disorderly motions of passion and bodily desire
need to be controlled and attuned in *Sophrosyne*
—temperance, self-control, right-mindedness,
wisdom.

Finally, the human soul is not unrelated to
surrounding Nature. Pythagoras taught the
doctrine implied in transmigration, that there is
a unity of all living things—that gods, men, and
animals form one community, animated by a
single principle of life which can pass from one
form to another. The soul is indestructible; and
according to its success or failure in achieving
harmony in itself and with the world, it is destined, in other lives, to rise or sink in the scale of
existence. On this earth the soul can reach the
threshold of divinity, and thereafter escape from
further incarnation. Regaining unalloyed perfection, it will dwell in the company of the im-

mortal gods, revisiting the earth no more. Man can become divine, because the life within him is a spark of the divine fire irradiating the universe.

It is not hard to imagine the effect of contact with such a philosophy upon the mind of Plato, already imbued with the Socratic morality of aspiration. He has allowed us a glimpse of that effect in a short dialogue, the *Meno*, which opens the series of the middle group. Pythagoreanism suggested to Plato the doctrine of Reminiscence, here announced as a solution of the problem of knowledge. Reminiscence, moreover, implies an immortal soul that can remember knowledge once possessed and forgotten.

The problem this doctrine is to solve may be stated as the question, how we can ever attain to a knowledge of those Forms or Ideals which Socrates was always trying to define. We cannot, for example, collect the meaning of perfect Justice from an examination of all the kinds of actions or institutions that different men and different communities call 'just'. No one of these actions or institutions is a complete embodiment of Justice, universally recognised as such. Perfect Justice is not a common character pervading them all, and capable of being abstracted or distilled out of a study of the whole collection. How, then, can we ever know that there is such a thing, if no

instance is to be found in experience? Or, if
such an instance were to be found, how could we
ever recognise it among all the other things
which bear the name of Justice without deserving
it? When we set out to seek a definition of Justice,
must we not (in some sense) already know the
thing we are looking for? But if we know it,
what need is there to look for it?

The theory of Reminiscence replies that knowledge of the perfect Forms, and indeed all knowledge of truth and reality, is at all times present
in the soul itself. The knowledge is there, but
latent and unconscious. What is called 'learning',
or the discovery of truth, is the recollection of
this latent knowledge, raised to the level of consciousness. The soul is guided in the search by
its own dim vision of a truth that is always present,
needing only to be seen more clearly, and co-
ordinated with other parts of the whole system of
Truth. Also, if knowledge is at all times present
to the soul, the soul must be immortal and independent of the body and its senses. It has seen
all truth in some former state of existence before
it came into the body. The truth has been forgotten, but it is stored in a memory from which
it can be recovered. This memory is not what we
commonly call the memory, not a register of the
experience which flows in, during this bodily

life, through the channels of sense. Its contents are impersonal, the same in all human beings, and they have never been extracted or distilled out of sensible experience.

In the *Meno* Plato represents Socrates as putting this theory to the test of experimental proof. He takes a slave who has never been taught geometry, and, solely by means of questions, elicits from him the solution of a not very easy problem of construction. Socrates claims that he has not told the slave anything: he has only asked him questions, and so led him on to see for himself the wrongness of his first attempts at solving the problem, and the rightness of the true solution.

It is here for the first time recognised that knowledge of mathematical truth is *a priori*. Plato would have seen a more striking confirmation in the experience of Pascal. When Pascal was a child, his father was afraid that his passion for abstract sciences might interfere with his learning Latin and Greek, and accordingly never permitted any discussion of mathematics in his presence. All the boy was allowed to know of geometry was that it had to do with the properties of figures and the extension of bodies in three dimensions. The child, in the privacy of his own room, set about discovering geometry for himself. With a piece of charcoal he traced on

the floor the shapes of triangles and parallelo-
grams, whose very names he did not know. He
was not yet twelve years old when he had made
out the definitions and axioms he required; and
he had reached the 32nd proposition of the First
Book of Euclid before he was detected and for-
bidden to discover the rest of geometry. Pascal's
unaided intelligence was able, from the mere contemplation of a diagram, to work, both upwards
to first principles, and downwards to more com-
plex propositions. The knowledge was not put
into his mind by a teacher, but drawn out of the
mind by its own exercise of intuition and deductive reasoning.[1]

The whole process is possible because the
objects upon which the mind is working—the
figures of geometry—are what Plato calls intelligible (as distinct from sensible) objects. 'The
Triangle', for instance, as defined by Euclid, is
not a diagram drawn in charcoal or a three-
cornered object that you can touch. No such
object is bounded by perfectly straight lines. The
best diagram or model you could actually make
in tangible material would always be irregular
and imperfect. It would also possess 'accidental'
qualities. The area would be of a certain size,

[1] If this anecdote is not true, it is enough for our
purpose that it might conceivably be true.

the sides of a certain length, which are accidental and irrelevant to the nature of the Triangle itself. Indeed, no visual image of the Triangle can even be conceived. Any triangle you picture to your mind must be either equilateral, or isosceles, or scalene; it cannot be all these at once. 'The Triangle' is not determined in any of these three specific ways. You can form no sensible image of this purely intelligible object. It is knowable; for its whole nature can be completely defined in terms already known. And it is perfect —an ideal transcending all the imperfect likenesses that our senses see or touch in the surfaces of material bodies. Thus the world of mathematical truth is an intelligible world, beyond the range of the bodily senses. When the soul withdraws from the senses to think by itself, it can travel freely in the region of this unseen reality. Intuition and deductive reasoning can advance from truth to truth, for every truth is linked to every other by the chain of logical necessity. We not only know each fresh truth with certainty; we know also why it must be true. This is knowledge in the complete sense. Unlike opinion or belief, it is perfectly clear and consistent; and it cannot be shaken by any persuasion from without.

Thus, in Plato's theory of Reminiscence, as in the Pythagorean philosophy, our knowledge of the perfect concepts and truths of mathematics is linked with the belief in a perfectible immortal soul. Plato saw, moreover, that the objects of mathematical knowledge are of the same order of intelligible reality as the objects of Socratic knowledge—those ideals of moral perfection which are to regulate the conduct of life. He claims for both the same independent and substantial existence beyond the flow of transitory things and temporal events. And the soul that knows them is by native right a denizen of that real world. The soul is always at home there; and thither it can at any time escape from the distractions of material existence and the importunities of the body with its senses and desires. Death is nothing but the complete detachment of the immortal soul from the body; and the life of the lover of wisdom is a rehearsal or preparation for that final deliverance. Such is the theme of the *Phaedo*, where two strands of argument are intertwined—the reality of the ideal Forms, independent of sensible things, and the reality of the soul, independent of its bodily habitation.

I am convinced that the doctrine of immortality developed in the *Phaedo* was never taught by Socrates. It is not consistent with what Socrates says in the *Apology* about the prospect of survival after death. Socrates' attitude there is agnostic.

His only claim to wisdom, he says, is that he does not imagine he knows what he does not know; and of what happens after death he knows nothing. Death may be a dreamless sleep; and that would be a gain, for a man could easily count the days of life he had spent more pleasantly than a night of sleep untroubled by dreams. Or it may be a migration of the soul into some Hades, where Socrates might hope to meet the great poets and the heroes of Troy. In that case, he would spend his time examining them, to find out which of them thought himself wise when he was not. In that world, at any rate, he could not be put to death for thus pursuing his mission; 'for the dead are immortal, if what we are commonly told is true'.

This passage occurs in an otherwise serious address to the judges, after the vote of condemnation. Socrates speaks of the alternative of annihilation in a tone of grave melancholy; he turns the prospect of survival into a joke that would have raised a burst of laughter in the court. Plato, writing the *Apology* years after Socrates was dead, could have no motive for misrepresenting or disguising his real attitude to the question of immortality. But, when he came to write the *Phaedo*, he had himself become convinced that the soul not merely survives the death of the body, but is an eternal and indestructible essence. He had also discovered the world of Forms containing the moral Ideals and the objects of mathematical knowledge, themselves eternal and indestructible essences, akin to the soul that knows them. In the light of these discoveries the death of Socrates, the perfect lover of wisdom, became a symbol for the death of every man. Death is neither annihilation, nor the migration to an Homeric Hades. It is the deliverance of the divine spirit in man from the prison-house of the flesh, where it has sojourned only as a stranger and pilgrim. In the *Phaedo*, Plato uses the recognised freedom of an imaginary conversation to put this new conception into the mouth of Socrates himself. He was justified in doing so, because he saw his own philosophy as a legitimate prolongation of Socrates' thought. The immortal spirit called 'the soul' in the *Phaedo* is identified with that 'true self' which Socrates had discovered—the reasonable self which aspires to spiritual perfection. Happiness, Socrates had believed, is attainable in this life in proportion as the true self advances towards perfection and takes control. Plato is more doubtful whether perfection of any sort can ever be reached in the world of time; but he is certain that perfection is realised in a world beyond time, not in the future, but in the eternal present.

Platonism goes beyond Socrates also in extending the philosophy of aspiration from the field of human life and conduct to the interpretation of the whole of Nature. We have already seen how the entire province of mathematical truth was annexed to the realm of intelligible Forms. How much further the boundaries of this realm are to be extended, is a question which Plato never answers with decisive clearness. It seems certain, indeed, that any elements in our experience of the material world which are not amenable to mathematical treatment are below the level of knowledge. Outside mathematics, there is no physical science of inanimate matter. In this field Plato follows out the consequences of Pythagoras' discovery. In the animal kingdom, however, living creatures, whose bodies are united with souls, exhibit in their structure certain forms or types, which appear to be constant and well defined. The word 'species', which we still use, is only the Latin translation of the Greek *eidos*, Plato's name for his eternal Forms. In its original use, the 'species' does not mean the whole assemblage of individuals of a given kind; it means the constant form, common to all the individuals, and more or less adequately embodied in each. If we watch the process of growth unfolding from the seed into the fully developed

plant with flower and fruit, we get the irresistible
impression of a mysterious impulse of life,
pushing its way, unerringly, in a predetermined
direction. We cannot conceive that the end of
this movement is foreseen by the individual plant
from the beginning; yet the result is as if the
end had all along been the goal of an unconscious
desire. The movement as a whole cannot be
accounted for by the interplay of material particles
colliding in space under mechanical impulsion.
Such causes can no more produce a rose tree than
a man could produce a dialogue of Plato by
striking the keys of a typewriter at random. It is
here that the Atomist philosophy breaks down in
ludicrous failure. Here too the Socratic idea of
aspiration comes to the rescue and enters into
the interpretation of Nature. The predetermined
movement of life seems to become intelligible
when we conceive the process as governed by the
end towards which it moves. The specific Form
can be thought of as an ideal of perfection and the
characteristic movement of life as an impulse of
desire. The Form of the species will then take
its place in the world of eternal reality, as the
ideal limit to which the individuals approximate,
or the perfect model of which they are imperfect
likenesses.

It is easy for a mechanistic philosophy to retort: 'All this is nothing but the recrudescence of rank anthropomorphism. You are importing into the interpretation of non-human nature a mechanism whose whole meaning and content is confined to the conduct of conscious and rational beings. Man's soul is capable of foreseeing and desiring an end; his actions are rightly explained as guided by purpose. But below the level of human consciousness, what sense can there be in talking of ends that are not foreseen and therefore cannot be desired? Where is the intelligence that is the seat of this desire or aspiration? If you cannot point to such an intelligence in Nature, your whole theory of ideals and final causes falls to the ground'.

Plato's reply is to be read in the *Timaeus*. It is frankly religious, and presented in the form of what the Greeks called a 'myth'. The *Timaeus* contains the myth of creation, a poetical statement of truth, not to be taken in its literal sense. The world, this dialogue tells us, can only be understood as the work of design, aiming at ideal perfection. The intelligence is the mind of the divine Artificer, who, being good, desires to produce a work that shall be, so far as possible, like himself. The perfect Forms are the model or pattern, with reference to which he fashions the universe in the conditions of space and time. The universe itself is a living creature, with a soul as well as a body—not a lifeless chaos of material atoms swept by the aimless winds of Chance. The soul of the world is attuned by the proportions and numbers of musical harmony; its body is limited and framed by geometrical form.

No doubt, this myth of creation is not to be taken at its face value; but interpreters who seek to penetrate beneath the surface and reduce Plato's poetry to something that men of science will accept as rational, run the risk of sacrificing what made it seem to Plato worth while to write the *Timaeus*. In the dialogues, he published to the world some of his essays after truth, in a tentative form which he hoped would not be misleading. They are mainly intended as examples of co-operative inquiry, suggesting further thought; not as a statement of attained results. When he approaches the ultimate mysteries he falls into figurative language. In one of his letters, he explicitly says that these mysteries cannot be expressed in speech or writing, and ought not to be so expressed, if they could. What seemed to him of imperative practical importance was that men who could never be philosophers should be persuaded to believe in a God who is not indifferent to the affairs of mankind, and to believe in an after life not unaffected by

the good or evil that is done on earth. Plato,
moreover, was prepared to impose these beliefs,
by the authority of the philosophic ruler, upon
the whole of society. In his commonwealth the
preacher of materialistic atheism would have been
offered the alternative of conversion or death.
Religion was to be taught to the unphilosophic
citizen in mythical form.

From first to last, the mainspring of Platonism
is its moral and political motive. When Plato
died, he was still at work upon the *Laws*, his
latest scheme for the reform of society. The
Socratic morality, reinterpreted under Pythagorean influence and expanded into a system of
the universe, had now become part of a religion
whose ultimate truths were accessible only to the
highly trained philosopher. And the philosopher
who has achieved wisdom is to govern his fellow-
citizens. This means that Socrates' ideal of self-
rule for every individual enlightened by self-
knowledge is once more to yield place, save for
a few individuals, to the external authority of the
wise over the unwise. When Plato projected his
reform of actual society and laid down its institutions, he was attempting to incorporate the
new morality of aspiration in a reformed morality
of social constraint. If only a few men can
become philosophers, the rest must be taught to

do as they are told. Self-knowledge and self-rule are not for them.

From that point of view, Plato's aristocratic commonwealth appears, not as an ultimate ideal for mankind, but as a compromise, which he hoped might prove to be just within the bounds of practical realisation. The hope was never to be fulfilled. In the Peloponnesian War, the fabric of moral life in the Greek city-state had been undermined and rent by the passions let loose in the turmoil of war and revolution. Plato could not see (as we can see from the course of later history) that the dissolution was beyond repair. The life which had flowed into that political form had come to the height of its climax in the Athens of Pericles. The city-state in Greece had no future, save the long catastrophe that began with the war.

Nor was that particular form of polity adequate to contain the spirit discovered by Socrates. The new morality was a universal morality. The life genuinely inspired by it demands, for its political frame, a world-wide organisation, co-extensive with the human race. It cannot be arrested at the boundaries of the city-state, nor yet of the nation. In the next century, after the conquests of Alexander, the Stoics began to perceive this truth. Their ideal of the wise man—the self-

ruling and free individual—was derived from
Socrates, rather than Plato; and they were the
first to understand that the wise man is a citizen
of the universe. The soul discovered by Socrates
cannot pay allegiance to the laws of any city
narrower than the city of Zeus.

Chapter IV

ARISTOTLE

Attracted to Athens by the fame of Plato, Aristotle came from his home in northern Greece in his eighteenth year to become a student of the Academy. Plato was then sixty and had been head of the school for at least fifteen years. No young student has ever been subject to the dominance of a more overpowering personality. Aristotle, of course, became a Platonist, and remained at the Academy for the next twenty years, as the pupil and then as the colleague of Plato, till Plato's death in 347 B.C. In imitation of his master, he wrote dialogues intended, like Plato's own earlier works, for the educated public throughout the Greek world. They were read and admired for centuries after his death; but they have not come down to us. We possess only enough fragments, preserved by other writers, to show us that Aristotle, in this first period of his career, was a whole-hearted Platonist, accepting the theory of ideal Forms, which he was afterwards to renounce.

When Plato died, the headship of the Academy passed to his nephew Speusippus, a man of no marked originality. We have no record of Aristotle's feelings upon the promotion of a colleague immeasurably inferior to himself. We only know that he left Athens with Xenocrates, who was later to succeed Speusippus, and that his attitude towards the Academy, and even towards Platonism, became increasingly antagonistic. If Aristotle ever strikes the modern reader as stupid— even wilfully stupid—it is where he has occasion to criticise the doctrines of Plato. There is no ground for attributing this tone to any personal resentment. Aristotle never ceased to reverence his master; and the founder of the Lyceum had no reason to envy the contemporary heads of the Academy. At the root of this antagonism lies a fundamental incompatibility of temperament; and a philosopher's temperament has more to do with the shaping of his philosophy than he would care to acknowledge, even if he were aware of the fact. Plato was (in the language of modern psychology) an introvert; and his philosophy is, in the end, a philosophy of withdrawal from the world of common experience. Platonism distrusts and condemns the senses. The eyes and ears are not, for the Platonist, windows of the soul, opening upon reality. The soul sees best when these windows are closed and she holds silent converse with herself in the citadel of thought. The native bent of Aristotle's mind was in the other direction, towards the study of empirical fact. His impulse was to explore the whole field of experience with insatiable curiosity. It is not hard to understand that a born man of science should have felt some measure of hardly conscious irritation at having been so long held in thrall by a philosopher whose thought, however magnificent, was radically uncongenial.

Aristotle and Xenocrates withdrew to Assos in the Troad, where they found friends in three former students of the Academy, one of whom was ruler of the city of Atarneus. Aristotle married his niece, Pythias. The marriage was a happy one; his will directs that they shall be buried in the same grave. In 343 B.C. Philip of Macedon invited him to superintend the education of Alexander the Great, then a child of thirteen. Philip may have known Aristotle as a boy; for Aristotle's father, Nicomachus, had been physician at the court of Macedonia.

In this second period of his life Aristotle's natural bent of mind was beginning to free itself from the authority of Plato. Fragments remain to us of a dialogue *Concerning Philosophy*, which may have been the programme of Aristotle's teaching at Assos. Here, for the first time, the Platonic doctrine of Forms is openly attacked, especially in its latest and most Pythagorean phase, in which the Forms were identified with the Ideal Numbers of a divine arithmetic, distinct from the numbers of mathematics. The denial of the world of Forms is the central point of Aristotle's dissent from Platonism. He will not admit that the ideal Forms can have any real existence, apart from the visible and tangible things which embody them. Nor will he admit that the objects of mathematical science are anything more than abstractions, made by our minds. The figures of geometry, for example, are simply the spatial attributes of actual bodies, considered in abstraction from their other properties. To Aristotle's mind (as to common sense) it seems obvious that the substantial reality of things must reside in the things themselves. It cannot be placed in another and higher order of entities, subsisting eternally in their own right, above the stream of time and change, indifferent to the very existence of the transitory things we see around us. The cosmology of the dialogue *Concerning Philosophy* remains markedly religious in tone. But the mythical creator of the *Timaeus*, and the divine model by which his work is guided, have disappeared. The world is without beginning or end. It is not a fleeting likeness of unchanging reality; this world itself is real and substantial. Aristotle is a man of this world, with no longing to escape

from it into another. On the contrary, he is
always trying to get back to this world, to escape
from the otherworldliness of Platonism, and to
regain contact with the philosophy of common
sense. The field of knowledge, awaiting his eager
exploration, lies within Nature as revealed by the
senses. The path of knowledge must start from
the evidence our senses give us, and must return
to it again, with a fuller understanding that will
justify the facts of observation.

It is characteristic of Aristotle to approach his
subject, in any branch of speculation, by starting
from the received opinions of ordinary men as
well as of philosophers. He remarks somewhere
that a man who ignores all that is commonly
believed or has been asserted by men of exceptional powers of thought, is not likely to hit upon
anything better. He even suspected that current
thought preserved relics of ancient wisdom which
had survived catastrophes, like Deucalion's
flood, that had from time to time overwhelmed
civilisation. Common sense, at any rate, is always
in close touch with practical experience. Its
beliefs, however blundering and confused, are
likely to contain some apprehension of truth that
can be distilled by criticism, and remodelled in
logical and coherent form.

Yet, for all this reaction towards the standpoint of common sense and empirical fact, Aristotle could never cease to be a Platonist. His thought, no less than Plato's, is governed by the idea of aspiration, inherited by his master from Socrates—the idea that the true cause or explanation of things is to be sought, not in the beginning, but in the end. Aristotelian philosophy remains a philosophy of final causes.

I cannot here attempt to outline the system of a man whose enormous industry, rivalled only, perhaps, by that of St Thomas, raised every problem that ingenuity could suggest, and pursued the solution to the smallest detail. In his school the main branches of Natural Science were, for the first time, recognised as departmental fields of inquiry, alongside the mathematical sciences developed by the Pythagoreans and Plato, with Logic and Metaphysics in the background. It has been estimated that in the *Encyclopaedia Britannica* (so long, at any rate, as that remained a work of Britannic scholarship) Aristotle occupied more pages than any other individual man; because there is no main subject of philosophy or science on which he had not said something still worth the hearing. I can only follow up the train of thought which started from the revolution in philosophy effected by Socrates, and dwell on the point that the idea of aspiration is still at the heart of the Aristotelian philosophy, even when it has broken away from the Idealism of Plato.

Aristotle's thought is at its best in the biological treatises and in the *Ethics*. The reason is that a philosophy of final causes is most illuminating in the study of animal life and of the moral nature of man. A modern man of science would probably think that the biological works contain more of enduring value than the rest of the Aristotelian Corpus. Darwin, at any rate, who possessed the noble gift of admiration, refers to them in terms almost more affectionate than respectful.[1] We shall find the kernel of Aristotle's thought in these books of natural history. They are characteristic

[1] To Dr Ogle (Feb. 22, 1882): "From quotations which I had seen, I had a high notion of Aristotle's merits, but I had not the most remote notion what a wonderful man he was. Linnæus and Cuvier have been my two gods, though in very different ways, but they were mere schoolboys to old Aristotle. How very curious, also, his ignorance on some points, as on muscles as the means of movement. I am glad that you have explained in so probable a manner some of the grossest mistakes attributed to him. I never realised, before reading your book, to what an enormous summation of labour we owe even our common knowledge."
Life and Letters of Charles Darwin, iii, 252.

products of the school he founded at Athens in the last period of his life, when he had finished Alexander's education. Some buildings rented in the Lyceum were converted to the purposes of a university. There was a large library with a collection of maps and a museum of objects to illustrate the lectures. Aristotle discoursed to his students on the more abstruse subjects in the morning and gave popular courses to a wider public in the afternoon. When they were not attending lectures and discussions, the students were occupied in research. They were set to the task of amassing collections of facts in human and natural history. The biological treatises contain, besides some theoretical speculation, a very considerable mass of detailed results of observation. The structure and habits of animals and plants are described, together with information gathered from hunters and fishermen. The information is not always correct; but on the other hand certain curiosities of marine biology were learnt from the Mediterranean fishermen, which have only been rediscovered, from the same sources, within living memory.

This science of observation and description was a new thing in the Greek world. Nothing earlier can be compared with it, except the clinical records of cases compiled by Hippocrates and his

Coan school of medicine. From the introduction to the treatise on the *Parts of Animals*, we can infer that young men accustomed to abstract discussions of moral philosophy and rhetoric were frankly disgusted when they were told to study the anatomy of reptiles and the repulsive habits of insects. Aristotle's exhortation to overcome these feelings is worthy of a man of science in any age:

> It remains to treat of the nature of living creatures, omitting nothing, whether of higher or lower dignity. For even in the case of creatures, the contemplation of which is disagreeable to the sense, Nature, who fashioned them, nevertheless affords an extraordinary pleasure to anyone with a philosophic disposition, capable of understanding causes. We take delight in looking at representations of these things, because we observe at the same time the art of the painter or sculptor which created them; and it would be strange that the contemplation of the works of Nature should not yield a still greater satisfaction, when we can make out their causes. Hence, the consideration of the lowlier forms of life should not excite a childish repugnance.

There is a story that, when some strangers who wished to meet Heracleitus stopped short on finding him warming himself at the kitchen stove, he told them to come boldly in, for 'there also there were gods'. In the same spirit we should approach the study of every form of life without disgust, knowing that in every one there is something of Nature and of beauty. For it is in the works of Nature above all that design, in contrast with random chance, is manifest; and the perfect form which anything born or made is designed to realise, holds the rank of beauty.

'The perfect form which the works of Nature are designed to realise' is the specific Form of the living creature. Such Forms, as we have seen, constitute that element in the economy of living Nature which has the best claim to rank with the mathematical and moral Forms in Plato's intelligible world. Considered as a type of perfection, the Form of the species is a goal, towards which the moving force of life seems to aspire. Biology is, in fact, the department of Natural Science in which the most hard-bitten believer in mechanical necessity has never been able to refrain from the language of final causes. The structure and essential peculiarities of a tool—a hammer or a saw—can only be understood and explained by the purpose the tool is made for. The same is true of those living tools or 'organs' which are parts of the living creature. It would be hard to find anywhere an account of the structure of the eye which did not imply that the eye was intentionally designed for the purpose of seeing. The explanation of the structure lies in the function or activity for the sake of which the eye exists. And the life history of the organism as a whole seems to be directed, from the outset, by a prevision of the form that is the actual outcome. The acorn, if nothing hinders its growth, develops without fail into an oak tree. The impulse of life within it never takes a wrong turn that would lead to a fir tree or a beech. Common sense, untroubled by philosophic doubts, is content to see in this process something more than a mere analogy to the working of a mind conscious of an end foreseen and desired.

On the other hand, we do not credit an acorn with conscious—or even unconscious—intelligence and foresight. Where is the mind that steers the movement so unerringly? Why does the force of life run, like a fluid, into just these constant moulds of form, each with its essential character, clearly marked off from the rest by a gulf that is not bridged by ambiguous and intermediate forms? Platonic theology had its mythical apparatus of the divine artist, fashioning the order of Nature, after the pattern of a perfect model, which includes the Forms of animal species. But Aristotle has renounced this expedient: he denies the separate existence of ideal Forms, and with the disappearance of the model, the creator too must disappear. Has, then, Nature herself a soul, dreaming, at some mysterious level of sub-consciousness, of an end that beckons and evokes the response of movement? Aristotle, not seldom, falls into language suggesting some such picture of a personified Nature, who 'does nothing with-out a purpose', and yet is not a conscious agent. But he is aware that such language is as mythical as the theology of the *Timaeus*. The man of science, the biologist, must call back his thoughts to the world of indubitably existing substances— the world of experience. Here, in these living things which are born and grow and reproduce their kind, he has before him the heart and centre of reality, if only he can divine the secret of their organisation.

Aristotle's characteristic contribution to the problem in question is the concept of potentiality. Men of science still cannot get on without the notion of 'potential energy'. Both words are terms to which Aristotle first gave currency. The recognition of potential energy keeps intact the principle of the conservation of energy, which is itself one application of the ancient doctrine that nothing can come out of nothing. The first article in the creed of science is that there must be no absolute becoming out of nothing at all, no absolute perishing into nothing at all. When the principle is applied to energy, it means that energy which ceases to exist in a manifest form must continue to exist in a form that is not manifest, but latent; it must exist potentially. An existence which is not actual might be suspected as no better than an arbitrary fiction invented to bolster up the principle of conservation. Experience, however, seems to confirm its validity. The sceptic who enters a magazine with a box of matches, determined to disprove the potentiality of explosive force in a barrel of powder, will not live to make his recantation. The warrant for the reality of potential existence is the fact that the energy which has ceased to be manifest and vanished into latency, can be manifested again. There is a power in the coiled spring that is stored in motionless inactivity but can be deployed in the actual movement of the hands of a watch, when you set it going.

Now if we apply this conception of potentiality to our biological problem, we shall say that the Form of the oak tree exists potentially in the acorn. The acorn *can* become an oak, and cannot become any other tree. In this way we shall escape the abhorrent notion of an absolute beginning of existence. The end will be implicit in the beginning, and will expand and flower into actuality. We shall cease to think of 'matter' as inert and passive body, awaiting the imposition of form from without, or as like the atoms of Democritus, lumps of impenetrable solidity, only to be moved by the shock of collision. Matter is not simply like the steel of which the spring is made; it is like the coiled spring in which the latent power of movement is stored. Aristotle defines a natural object as a thing that has a source of motion in itself. Even the simple bodies (as he called them)—Fire, Air, Earth, and Water—possess each an inherent tendency to move towards its proper region—Fire upwards, Earth downwards. And in the living creature this inherent power of motion can be attributed to the Form itself, whether its existence be at the potential or at the actual stage. In the process of reproduction the 'moving cause' is commonly identified by Aristotle with the specific Form actually realised in the fully developed parent; but in the act of generation this Form is communicated to the new individual, and, with it, is transmitted the force or power that will carry the process of development once more from the potential phase to the actual. Thus the specific Form travels through an unending series of individuals. It is the bearer of a life that is immortal in time, though each individual perishes when it has been born, has grown to full development, and has given birth to a successor.

In this way the Platonic Form of the species is brought down from its heaven of unchanging reality, and plunged in the flow of time and sensible existence. It seemed to Aristotle that so long as the Form was conceived as having a separate eternal existence in full realisation, it could have no power of calling likenesses of itself into being. The Platonic ideal Form was to him a superfluous and idle hypothesis. The concept of potentiality enabled him to describe the observed processes of life, without (as he thought) invoking 'poetical metaphors', or building a world of ideal reality to overarch the stream of temporal becoming.

For all that—to go back to our main point— this biological science is inspired, no less than Platonism, by the idea of aspiration. The complete Form is an end, not only in the sense that it is the last stage of a process of development, but also in the sense that it is a 'good' or perfection; and the movement of life towards its realisation is like the movement of human desire towards the goods we wish for. Biology is the field in which the apparatus of concepts we have reviewed—Aristotelian Form and Matter, the actual and the potential—is most at home and

most illuminating. And it might be expected that
Aristotle, having ousted from this field the un-
necessary hypothesis of a divine creator and his
model, would complete his system without re-
quiring a God of any sort. But when he passes
beyond biology to the whole range of physical
science, he cannot dispense with a God; and this
God is precisely the ultimate goal of aspiration.
So deeply is this idea rooted in Aristotle's mind
that it is invoked to account for all motion and
change in Nature. The cause or reason, not only
of the movement of life, but of all movement
whatsoever, is to be found, not in the beginning,
but in the end. In relation to the world as a
whole, the name for that end is 'God'—the pure
and supreme Form, which moves all things, not
by mechanical impulsion, but by attraction, as the
object of desire.

The argument demonstrating the existence of
such a being is unconvincing to a modern scientific
mind, and strikes a chill to the religious consciousness. It may be summarised as follows.
Substances are the first of existing things. Therefore, if substances are perishable, all things are
perishable. But change and time are not perishable: they can never have begun to exist, nor
can they cease. Now the only change that can be
continuous and unending is circular motion in

space. There must, then, be an eternal circular motion; and to produce and sustain such motion, there must be an eternal substance, whose essence is not power but activity, and which is therefore a pure immaterial Form. Now, experience shows us that there exists an eternal circular motion, namely the revolution of the heaven of the fixed stars. What moves that heaven? It must be something that causes motion, without itself being moved. This unmoved mover can only be that pure and active Form whose existence has been demonstrated. The activity of this Form must be of the highest kind conceivable—an eternal life of self-contemplation, for the only object adequate to God's contemplation must be God himself. Being perfect he desires nothing; but because he is perfect, he is the object of the world's desire, and so the ultimate cause of the physical motion of the revolving spheres, and in the sublunary region, of the movement of all forms towards their own realisation.

The assertion that God's activity must be thought or contemplation is manifestly deduced from the doctrine that contemplative rational thought is the highest activity known to man. After a description of the Prime Mover, Aristotle continues:

On such a principle depend the heavens and the

world of Nature. And its life is such as the best that
we enjoy, though we enjoy it for but a short time....The
act of contemplation is what is most pleasant and best.
If, then, God is always in that good state in which
we sometimes are, this compels our wonder; and if
in a better, this compels it yet more. And God *is* in
a better state. Life also belongs to God; for the
actuality of thought is life, and God *is* that actuality....
We say, therefore, that God is a living being, eternal
and most good; so that life and duration, continuous
and eternal, belong to God; for this *is* God.

The activity of the divine thought is contemplative, not practical; self-contained, not issuing
in action. God has no operation upon the world,
nor even a knowledge of the world. The conception of this divine activity is plainly derived
from its counterpart in man. The *Ethics* teaches
that the end of man is the perfect exercise of the
highest function essential to our nature; and this
is finally identified with the activity of that divine
rational self which Socrates had discovered and
Plato had declared to be immortal. This reason
or spirit has no bodily organ, no material accom-
paniment. It is, indeed, sometimes active in
practical wisdom, directing conduct; but such
practical activity is a means to an end beyond
itself, whereas theoretical activity is always an
end in itself, and therefore (Aristotle holds) of a

higher value. In this doctrine of a separate spirit
or reason, independent of the body, Aristotle's
fidelity to Platonism is once more conspicuous.
As a man of science, he had (so to say) no
business to believe in such a spirit, distinct from
the vital principle, or soul, which he declares to
be inseparable from the matter of the mortal
body it informs, and therefore itself mortal. The
separable immortal spirit is an article of faith,
inherited from Socrates and Plato, which Aristotle, perhaps, was too wise to sacrifice at the
altar of consistency. In his exaltation of theoretical above practical activity he is more Platonist than Plato; and it is this which leads him to
conceive a God who can neither know nor act
upon the universe, but is absorbed in the contemplation of himself.

It has always seemed to me unfortunate that
the word 'God' (which is, after all, a religious
word) should have been retained by philosophers
as the name for a factor in their systems that no
one could possibly regard as an object of worship,
far less of love. In the Middle Ages, the subtlety
of scholastic rationalism was strained to the
utmost in the attempt to reconcile Aristotle's
God with the God proclaimed in the Gospels.
As to the success of this attempt, I prefer to quote
the verdict of a Catholic philosopher. Don Miguel

de Unamuno,[1] after speaking of the God of the Old Testament, continues:

> Subsequently reason—that is, philosophy—took possession of this God who had arisen in the human consciousness as a consequence of the sense of divinity in man, and tended to define him and convert him into an idea. For to define a thing is to idealise it, a process which necessitates the abstraction from it of its incommensurable or irrational element, its vital essence. Thus the God of feeling, the divinity felt as a unique person and consciousness external to us, although at the same time enveloping and sustaining us, was converted into the idea of God.
>
> The logical, rational God, the *ens Summum*, the *primum movens*, the Supreme Being of theological philosophy...is nothing but an idea of God, a dead thing....
>
> The traditional so-called proofs of the existence of God all refer to this God-Idea, to this logical God, the God by abstraction, and hence they really prove nothing; or rather, they prove nothing more than the existence of this idea of God.

Such is the reaction of a profoundly religious mind to the Aristotelian element in Catholic divinity. The plain truth is that the Being described as the object of the world's desire, the goal of aspiration, has ceased to be an object that

[1] *The Tragic Sense of Life*, translated by J. E. Crawford Flitch (London, 1921), p. 159.

could excite anything recognisable as desire. When the God of feeling is rationalised into a logical abstraction, the feeling itself dwindles and fades into something of no more significance to religion than a force of attraction imagined as causing two material particles to gravitate together. By a curious turn of the wheel, the philosophy of aspiration ends with a God whose function, in relation to the world, is the same as that of the Intelligence in Anaxagoras' system. Socrates was disappointed when he found that Anaxagoras made no use of this Intelligence for any purpose save to initiate motion in space. He wanted a divine Intelligence which would plan the order of the world for the best. Plato's mythical theology met this demand; but Aristotle's God does not plan the order of the world, or work for any good end. He is himself the end, wrapt in the contemplation of his own perfection; and his influence on the world is really confined to causing the revolution of the outermost heaven of stars—a motion in space. It seems to matter little whether the Prime Mover be placed, with Anaxagoras, at the beginning, or, with Aristotle, at the end. The philosophy of aspiration has become an inverted mechanism. If Socrates could have read the *Metaphysics*, he would hardly have recognised the outcome of the new movement of thought he had himself originated.

To us it is evident that the life-blood of the morality of aspiration is not 'desire', attenuated to something barely distinguishable from mechanical attraction, but a more vital feeling. Let us keep to the Authorised Version and call it charity. Charity is the missing element which Dante and his teachers strove to fuse with the Aristotelian desire in that *Amor* which moves the sun and the other stars. But this element came from another quarter, and not even the genius of Dante can make the fusion plausible. Charity suffereth long; the one thing it will not suffer is rationalisation. The Aristotelian system, when it passes beyond the biological field to include the whole range of physics and metaphysics, is a colossal monument of rationalism, a compact and all-embracing structure furnished with an answer to every question. It is the fate of such a monument to become a cenotaph, not a permanent refuge for the spirit. The Greeks asserted the claims of the head, Christianity, the claims of the heart. Both claims are valid and complementary. The modern world, it may be admitted, sometimes needs to be reminded by the ancient that in a complete philosophy of life there is room for hard thinking as well as for feeling.

If charity is left out of account, the strength of the morality of aspiration lies in that other feature which distinguishes it from the morality of social constraint. Its centre is an ideal that has been incarnated in a great personality, whose life is the warrant that a perfection seldom realised is not beyond the extreme capacity of human nature. For the ancient world that personality was Socrates. From Socrates the two schools of Stoics and Epicureans, who confronted one another as rivals through the remaining centuries, both traced their descent. Both saw in him a man who had achieved that untroubled peace of mind which, in their several ways, they conceived as the secret of happiness.

The Epicurean is the more attractive, perhaps because the gentle Epicurus himself assigned a large place in the happy life to that form of charity which is known as friendship. He had no use for the frozen theology of Aristotle; and Plato's dogma of moral retribution in another world repelled and frightened him. He accepted the materialist philosophy of Atomism, not for its scientific merit, but for its assurance that the soul of man is *not* immortal, and need anticipate neither reward nor punishment after death. The certain hope of annihilation was to rob religion of its horrors. But such a hope is hard to distinguish

from despair, or at best from resignation. There
is an invincible melancholy in the Epicurean exhortation:

Come on therefore, let us enjoy the good things
that are present, and let us speedily use the creatures
like as in youth. Let us fill ourselves with costly wine
and ointments; and let no flower of the spring pass by
us. Let us crown ourselves with rosebuds before they
be withered. Let none of us go without his part of our
voluptuousness; let us leave tokens of our joyfulness
in every place; for this is our portion, and our lot is
this.

The Stoic would have none of these ambiguous
consolations. He is the puritan, holding to the
tradition of Socrates' cheerful indifference to
bodily pleasures, but disposed to mistake this
indifference for a rather grim and graceless as-
ceticism. He can see no distinction between trust
in providence and submission to fate. He
marches, in the filthy rags of righteousness, with
face set towards a peak of infallible wisdom and
virtue, which even the small company of the elect
have little or no hope to climb.

These later philosophies, however, are beyond
my province. I mention them because I cannot
resist the temptation to round off the analogy I
drew at an earlier stage. In pre-Socratic science
we saw something of the attitude of wondering

childhood; and in certain utterances of the Sophists we heard the accent of the adolescent rebellion against authority. In Socrates, Plato, and Aristotle, Greek philosophy grows to the maturity of responsible manhood and the fullness of intellectual power. But the extravagance of the intellect seems destined to overreach itself as surely as the extravagance of the myth-making imagination. Then nothing remains but the philosophy of old age, the resignation of a twilight that deepens alike over the garden of Pleasure and the hermitage of Virtue.

INDEX